ROBERT DARDEN

I, JESUS

*Stories from
the Savior*

THE SUMMIT PUBLISHING GROUP • ARLINGTON, TEXAS

THE SUMMIT PUBLISHING GROUP
One Arlington Centre
1112 East Copeland Road, Fifth Floor
Arlington, Texas 76011

Printed in the United States of America.

01 00 99 98 97 010 1 2 3 4 5

Library of Congress Cataloging-in-Publication Data

Darden, Bob, 1954-
    I, Jesus: stories from the Savior / by Robert Darden.
        p.   cm.
    ISBN 1-56530-185-4
    1. Jesus Christ—Biography. I. Title.
BT301.2.D37 1996
232.9'01—dc20
[B]   96-10103
                                                             CIP

Cover and book design by David Sims

I, JESUS

Dedicated to five pastors
who modeled the Living Christ for me:

LLOYD HELTON
RAYMOND PARKER
DANIEL BAGBY
MIKE MASSAR
RAYMOND BAILEY

CONTENTS

This book is an exercise in creative imagination.
What if there were only *one* gospel?
And what if it were written *today*?
What would be different?

The most obvious difference would be that there would be more background detail and more attention to setting and chronology. The writers of the Gospels weren't particularly interested in such things as motivation, individual characterization, background, and context. All four writers had important stories to tell and important points to make. But whether there was one blind man at the gate or two, whether it was the Sermon on the Mount or the Sermon on the Plain, whether Jesus cleansed the Temple once or twice—none of this really mattered that much to them. For me, on the other hand, these are the very sort of details that make pages come alive. So, while I accept the accounts I have found in scripture without feeling a need to revise or justify them in any way, I just cannot help but wonder about some of the things that aren't mentioned.

What I have done is retell, yet again, the greatest story ever told. I told it like *I* wanted to read it—from beginning to end. I wanted to know *where* Jesus was at any given time. I wanted to know *why* people like Simon the Zealot and Judas Iscariot did what they did. I wanted to know what the scenery was like so that I could picture myself there. I wanted to taste the dust and feel the hot sun.

I wanted to be there beside the Christ.

A special word of thanks is due to the following for their insight, encouragement, and invaluable assistance during the writing of *I, Jesus:*

Raymond Bailey
Blake Burleson
Mary Darden
Robert Darden, Jr.
JoAnn Darden
Rex Downie, Jr.
Tom Hanks
Mark Murphy
Len Oszustowicz
William R. Scott
Missy Tate
Lynn Tatum

—and to Jesus Christ, once of Nazareth, now and always our Risen Lord and Savior.

—Robert Darden

The Birth of a Messiah

THE BIRTH OF JOHN THE BAPTIST

"Mary, you have visitors."

"Oh John, I'm much too tired. It isn't that tax collector again, is it? Sometimes I think Ephesus has as many tax collectors as it has citizens."

"No. It is just some neighborhood children. I'll tell them to come back later."

"Children? Why didn't you say so? Send them in! Send them in!"

"Is it wise? You have been looking so thin and pale—"

But it was too late. A fistful of chattering children were already squeezing through the door, squealing merrily, making a beeline for Mary's room.

"—lately."

John smiled briefly, then returned to his brooding watch, scanning the town of Ephesus below.

Soon. It will be soon. The Romans will find us again and we will be forced to flee. Or I will be sent in exile. Or. . .or worse. And what of Mary then?

John looked back at Mary's room, the children clustered around her, each vying for her attention, each trying to sit closest to her. "Tell us the story again, Revered Mother! You promised! You always tell us the story at this time of year."

"What a good memory you have, Abibu. Surely you must be tired of the same story year after year."

"Oh no, Revered Mother. Each year it becomes more wonderful."

"I like the part about the magi, the wise men who came from so far away to find you."

"No, Naboth, you silly! The wise men came to find the *baby*. Isn't that right?"

"You win, my darlings. I will tell the story again.

"Oh, I remember, I remember—where you are betrothed to Joseph! And both of you are from the line of David!" Abibu said excitedly. But when he noticed all of the other children looking at him, his face flushed red and he quickly sank back to his knees.

"That's right, Abibu," Mary said. "I was just a girl, not quite fourteen. Joseph wasn't much older. But I loved him very much. He was very mature for his age. And very handsome, too.

"But one night an angel appeared to me! He was both beautiful and scary at the same time. It seemed like he was bigger than the whole room I was sitting in. You can imagine how frightened I was. He said his name was Gabriel."

For a moment, Mary pauses in her narrative, her eyes closed, remembering every detail.

"And...and he spoke to me. His voice was like quiet rolling thunder. He said, 'Greetings, Mary, you who are highly favored. The Lord is with you.'

"He must have seen me shaking with fear, so he said, 'Do not be afraid, you have found favor with God. You will be with child and give birth to a son and you will name him *Jesus*. He will be great and will be called the Son of the Most High. The Lord God will give him every throne of his father David and he will reign over the house of Jacob forever and his kingdom will never end!'

"I was shaking so hard, I didn't know what to say, what to do. I could still feel Gabriel's presence, even though I'd kept my eyes closed the entire time. At last, I peered up at him. I had to squint because a bright light was shining from him.

"I said, 'But I am a virgin. How will this be?'

"At first, I thought he was mad at me. I thought maybe he'd strike me down for questioning him. His beautiful face was troubled. Now I know that Gabriel wasn't angry—he was frightened. The most important message in history has just been given and he's telling it to a skinny little Nazarene girl shaking on her knees!

"But you don't get to be head angel by questioning the Lord. Gabriel smiled at me and said, 'The Holy Spirit will come upon you and the power of the Most High will cover you. And he will be called the Son of God. If Elizabeth has conceived, she who was barren for so long, do you doubt the power of God? Nothing is impossible with God!' "

All of the children listened, enraptured. Giant tears spilled down Mary's cheeks.

At last, Naboth spoke: "Please don't cry, Revered Mother. What did you do?"

Mary dried her eyes and mustered a smile.

"I said, 'I am the Lord's servant. May it all happen as you have said.' I bowed before Gabriel and when I looked back up, he was gone.

"But I knew, even then, that I was pregnant."

For the first time, John spoke.

"I'll wager Joseph wasn't too happy over that bit of news, Mary," he said, his eyes smiling.

"No, dear John, he wasn't," she said. "At first he was speechless, especially when I told him about the angel. Then he was sad. He...he made plans to end our engagement. I...I don't think he believed me and I'm not sure I blame him. He didn't want anyone to know. But he didn't speak to me again all that day.

"But that night, an angel appeared to Joseph as well. He assured Joseph it was all true. Then the angel said, 'All of this took place to fulfill what the Lord had said through the prophet: *The virgin will be with child and will give birth to a son and they will call him Immanuel—which means "God with us." ' *

"Wow! Did Joseph apologize the next day?" Abibu asked.

Mary flashed a crooked smile at John across the room.

"Well, precious one, sometimes it is difficult for men to apologize. But dear Joseph did—if not in so many words. And he never doubted me again."

Mary ran a pale hand across her brow. John, ever alert, reacted immediately.

"Mary is tired, children," he said. "We'll finish this another day."

He carefully lifted the sleeping Naboth into Abibu's arms and the children reluctantly filed out—but not before Mary had hugged each of them.

THE BIRTH OF JESUS

While Mary rested, John prepared their meager meal. After supper, they walked outside and sat under an ancient oak. The night sky was ablaze in light, uncounted stars flickering and dancing around a wan, pale moon.

At first, John thought Mary was sleeping. Then he noticed she was staring off into the star-studded night.

"It was on a night much like this, you know," she said, her voice barely above a whisper. John inched closer.

"It was a good time to be in Nazareth," she continued. "There was much work for Joseph. The Romans were always building something and Joseph—as you probably remember—was a master craftsman/builder. He all but had a monopoly on construction in Nazareth.

"But to pay for those splendid roads and villas, the Romans needed taxes. And when they needed taxes, they had another census."

"Oh, I remember that one," John said quietly. "Took ten years to complete. Herod was a stickler for details. Uprooted half the country. We all had to return to our hometowns and be counted. The roads were a nightmare; whole tribes of people in transit. They tell me one such Roman census in Gaul took forty years to complete!"

"It must be hard to count a people who don't want to be counted," Mary sighed. "But we complied, even though I was due any day and Joseph would lose a valuable construction job. We returned to Bethlehem. The roads were clogged every step of the way, and I felt every cobblestone all the way up my spine.

"To make matters worse, when we got to Bethlehem, there wasn't a room to be had anywhere. Neither of us had any family left in the village and the inns were full.

"I'm afraid we must have looked a pitiful sight to that last innkeeper. I was as big as a house and we were both covered with dust. He said that travelers were sleeping in the hallways and tents on the roof—there was simply no room for us.

"But he was a compassionate man and gave us a room in a small cave where he stabled the animals. He let Joseph sweep it up and bring in fresh straw. And with the little donkey and ox in their stalls, it was probably as warm in there as the rooms in the inn!"

"What do you remember of Jesus' birth?" John asked.

"Only that he seemed to be the most beautiful child in the world," Mary said dreamily. "Now I know that *all* newborn babies are the most beautiful children in the world to their parents."

"Did he cry?"

"Of course. Jesus was a normal baby. He cried, he slept, and sometimes I think he smiled.

"Sometime during the night, an angel appeared to several groups of shepherds out in the fields with their flocks, and then a great host of angels, all singing and telling them that a baby born that night in Bethlehem would be the Christ. I found out later that they left their sheep and combed the village, looking for a baby wrapped in cloths and lying in a manger.

"And John, when they finally found us, it was wonderful. It was a procession of shepherds of all ages, all tumbling in, all talking at once. They told me the most amazing stories of what they had seen in the heavens and what they had heard that night. They were dressed in rags and animal skins and they smelled of the fields and hills. And yet each stood wide-eyed and awed at the sight of my little baby. Old, wizened, scarred shepherds, fresh-eyed, curly-haired young shepherds—all of them praising God, all fumbling for the right words to say."

"What did they do after they left?" John asked.

"Why, they went throughout Bethlehem and the surrounding villages, telling people what they had seen."

"And what did the people of Bethlehem do?"

"Nothing," Mary said flatly. "No one came and visited us. No one offered us room. No one cared."

"No one?" John had never heard this part of the story before.

"I suppose the 'good' citizens of Bethlehem had trouble believing a band of ragged shepherds. Perhaps they thought they were drunk or something. But it does seem strange that among a people who had been waiting patiently for a Messiah for so long, no one could bestir themselves from their warm homes that night to see what all the commotion was about. But no one ever came."

John tenderly placed a hand on Mary's slight shoulder.

"Come. You must rest. The children will return tomorrow and you will want to be strong."

"Yes, of course you are right, dear John. I don't know what I would have done without you."

"You would have done what you've *always* done, Revered Mother. You would have been an inspiration to us all. Now stay here while I get the candle."

THE INFANT JESUS AT THE TEMPLE

The next day, John carefully helped Mary find a comfortable spot in the morning sun. As he arranged the blankets over her legs, she smiled her thanks.

"You are kind to look after an old woman like me, John. You need to tend to your own writing."

"It is my honor. It is not often one can be of service to the mother of our Lord and Savior."

But before Mary could finish her thought, they were interrupted by peals of silvery laughter resounding down the little path to their cottage.

"I fear we are about to be invaded, Mary."

"And never was there a more willing captive, John."

Soon a dozen children descended on the humble garden, attracted to Mary like bees to honey.

"Shush, shush, my darlings. I can't hear you if you all talk at once."

Little Naboth shyly stepped forward. "I picked this flower for you, Revered Mother."

"It is lovely, Naboth. Thank you. But I have nothing to give you in return."

"Oh, I want nothing in return. Though we always enjoy your stories, Revered Mother. *Particularly* those about the magi."

"Ah, you are a sly one. I would almost think young Abibu put you up to such a cunning plan."

"On my honor, Revered Mother," Abibu protested quickly, "I did no such thing."

"Then it is a story you shall have," Mary said gaily.

John could not help but smile himself.

When she laughs like that, she looks so young, so beautiful. It is as if, for a moment, she forgets all she has seen and endured in the last forty years.

Mary closed her eyes briefly in the warm morning sun and then began:

"I am told that shortly after we returned from Jerusalem, a caravan entered Jerusalem from the East. It must have been very large, for it contained supplies for a long trip and soldiers to defend it as it passed through the wild lands beyond the *Pax Romana*. When the leaders of this caravan paid a courtesy call to Herod to assure him of their peaceful intentions, I am told that he asked them, 'Why have you come?'

"They replied, 'We are looking for the one called king of the Jews. We saw his star in the east and have come to worship him. Do you know of him, O King?'

"Immediately, there was a great uproar in court and word spread through Jerusalem like wildfire. But crafty old Herod kept his counsel to himself. Remember children: here was a man who had had his sons and wives killed to protect his throne! So Herod only nodded and said, 'Allow me to assist you in some small way.'

"And he immediately summoned all of the chief priests and teachers of the Law. Within minutes, they appeared, from all over Jerusalem, breathless and flustered, to do Herod's bidding."

Mary stopped her narrative. "Do you know what they said, Abibu?"

"Yes, Honored Grandmother," he said proudly. "They quoted from the prophet Micah: *But you, Bethlehem, in the land of Judah, are by no means least among the rulers of Judah; for out of you will come a ruler who will be shepherd of my people Israel.*"

"Excellent, Abibu!" she said. "You attend your lessons well. That is exactly what they said.

"Herod dismissed the priests and teachers and called the magi into his chambers. He inquired of them the exact time the star appeared and sent them to Bethlehem. Then he said, 'Go and make a *careful* search for the child. As soon as you find him, report to me, so that I too may go and...*worship* him.' "

"Oooo, that liar!" Naboth exclaimed angrily. The other children laughed.

"When the wise men left Jerusalem, the star they had been following rose again and it led them directly to us. Imagine our surprise when this giant, sprawling royal caravan stopped outside our stable! And when the magi walked in and saw us, they dropped to their knees and worshiped Jesus! Joseph and I could scarcely believe our eyes and ears. And they presented us with wonderful gifts: gold, frankincense, and myrrh.

"The frankincense and myrrh are long gone, my children, but I still have a single piece of gold from that visit. Would you like to see it?"

The children gasped in unison and crowded around to see.

From a simple leather pouch she pulled a single, worn gold coin.

"It is from Babylon, long ago," Mary said. "One of the magi said it had belonged to Daniel, whose writings they still study and revere.

"And then we talked long into the night. They told us of the great city by the two rivers where they lived, of their perilous journey across the desert, of the strange star that appeared and disappeared for months on end—always leading them west.

"They also told us what Herod had said. Joseph and I were concerned, for we knew all too well of Herod's murderous rages and insane jealousy, but we said nothing to the magi.

"And then, after leaving us more gifts of food and gorgeous hand-crafted rugs, they pitched their tents for the night. Several times during the night, I got up just to wander through their camp. I loved looking at the strange colors and symbols, staring at the camels, and smelling the wonderful spices in their foods and incense. I felt completely safe with this sprawling caravan surrounding us."

Mary stopped once again, staring into the distance, lost in her memories. Naboth began to speak, but Abibu gently held a finger to the little boy's lips.

"She is remembering," he whispered. "It is good."

After a few moments, Mary shook herself, as if to awaken from a dream.

"Oh, I was daydreaming, wasn't I, children? Forgive an old woman, will you?"

"You were telling us about the wise men, Revered Mother," Naboth said respectfully.

"Oh yes, so I was. Before dawn the next morning, the leader of the caravan approached our stable again. I was already outside preparing breakfast. He was very tall and very handsome and his clothes were of the finest silk. He said, 'We have been warned in a dream not to return to Herod, for he wishes your child great harm. We shall instead return home by a different route.'

"While they were preparing to leave, Joseph awoke and came outside as well. He too had been warned by an angel to leave Bethlehem immediately.

"I said, 'But where shall we go? His soldiers will doubtless trace us back to our home in Nazareth.'

"Dear Joseph said, 'The angel has instructed us to flee to Egypt.'

"Believe you me, dear ones, I did not relish the prospect of a long, dangerous journey to Egypt with a tiny baby. But we had both learned by this point that it isn't wise to doubt angels! And that's when we left Bethlehem."

And then Mary looked lovingly at each child.

Abibu spoke first: "Thank you for telling us the story again, Revered Mother."

Little Naboth shyly reached up and gave Mary a kiss on the cheek and then fled out the door, the others in laughing pursuit. But Mary sat quietly, unmoving. When John drew closer, he noticed tears streaming down her cheeks.

Alarmed, he said, "Mary, what is the matter?"

"There is an ending to the story that I have never told the children, John, one that pains me to this day."

John sank to his knees and took Mary's hands. "What is it?"

"Eventually, when the magi did not return to Jerusalem, Herod flew into a rage. When his spies reported that the magi had already left his jurisdiction, he ordered his soldiers to Bethlehem. They...they slaughtered all of the boys under the age of two. More than a dozen innocent babies died that terrible day. Then he left strict orders that if anyone should mention this unspeakable massacre, he would have them killed as well."

John's face went ashen. "I...I had no idea."

"We did not hear of it until much later. Joseph found work in Egypt and there we stayed for a few months until another angel came to us one night and told us that the Romans' bloodthirsty puppet had died. The angel told us to return to Nazareth—and you know the rest of the story."

John nodded, his eyes never leaving Mary.

"But sometimes, late at night, my dreams are haunted by the cries of those precious babies," she said.

"You must not dwell on it, Mary. We will all see those blessed children some day when we are together in the bosom of Abraham."

"Yes, I suppose we shall. Still . . ."

"No more. Besides, it is getting warm out here in the sun. Let us go inside and prepare for our trip to market. Perhaps we can eat there."

CHAPTER ONE

My Father's Business

JESUS ANNOUNCES HIS DEPARTURE FROM HOME

A*nd then one day, the call came.*
I was at the ancient city of Sepphoris, not far from
Nazareth, finishing a construction project. I had grown up work-
ing under Romans at Sepphoris—who had destroyed it in their
original conquest, but were now rebuilding it as the capital of
Galilee for Herod Antipas.

I studied and worked there first with Joseph before he died,
then later with my brothers James, Joseph, Judas, and Simon.
Joseph trained us well. We were comfortable both with the carpenter's axe and the mason's mortar. Sepphoris had provided
employment for our family since I was a child. Now the recon-
struction was nearly complete and the Romans would be arriving.

And then the call came.

I walked back to Nazareth that afternoon in silence through
the rich and rolling Galilean countryside. James must have known
something was going on, but said nothing.

At home, my beloved mother and sisters were waiting for us.
The pots were bubbling and the hearth smelled of warm bread.

After dinner, I asked everyone to join me by the fire.

"Mother, I must leave. My time has come."

"Leave?" James spluttered. "Leave? But where? To do what? With our father gone, you are the head of the household. How can you leave? Mother, can he do that?"

Mother smiled that same sad smile I had seen so many times before.

"Of course he can, James. Jesus is thirty, a full-grown man. He has provided well for all of us since Joseph died. And, perhaps, someday soon all of you will leave as well."

I smiled back at her care-worn face and breathed a silent prayer of gratitude. *Thank you, Father. And thank you, dear mother, I knew you would understand.*

"I had been expecting this for some time," she continued, as the others looked on, their surprise still written across their faces. "Perhaps, in his love for us, Jesus stayed longer than he should have."

Simon stepped forward. "Where will you go?"

"I'm not sure, my friend. I feel compelled to see our cousin John first, then maybe I'll understand a little better."

"John?!" Simon said, now genuinely confused. "The Baptizer? The one that lives off of bugs in the desert and calls for repentance? *Our* John?"

"The very same. Something tells me he has a message for me as well."

"Is he really a wild man?" my youngest sister asked. "He sounds horrible—and scary!"

"John has had a difficult life," my mother said sternly. "His parents—and my beloved cousin Elizabeth—died when he was quite young. He was sent to live with the poor teachers who study and pray on the western shores of the Dead Sea. He dresses in camel skin because he's poor. And if he eats locust and wild honey, as they say, then it is because there is nothing else in that barren land. John deserves our love and pity—not scorn."

"Would you like for me to accompany you?" James asked, his hand on my shoulder.

"Thank you James, but no. You are needed here. You will be the head of the household."

"I'm sorry we have so little to give you, my son," Mary said, her eyes brimming with tears.

"Nonsense! You have given me a loving household, a warm place to sleep, excellent meals, a fine education—and a lifetime of love! I'll need only a bedroll—and perhaps just one or two loaves of your excellent bread in the morning. Is there a richer man in all of Galilee?"

With that, my sisters ran forward and we hugged and kissed each other. They peppered me with questions and we laughed and cried and told stories on each other.

JESUS SETS OUT ON HIS MISSION

The next morning, mother and I were the first up—as usual. As we fixed breakfast for the others, I said, "Mother, you've never told my brothers and sisters about all of the wonderful things you saw and heard in Bethlehem, have you?"

She shook her head.

"No, I didn't want them to treat you differently; I didn't want the others to resent you. Joseph and I agreed a long time ago to raise you like every other Galilean boy.

"And I know I've only ever mentioned those events to you once or twice—mostly for the same reason. And, perhaps, one other."

"What other reason, mother?"

"That I...that is, I still don't really understand what it all means, even now. The angels, the magi, the shepherds—I don't know what it all means for you, my son. Sometimes I'm not sure they ever really happened, and yet...I'm so confused."

"And yet you let me go today."

"That much I understood. That you have a mission, a God-given mission. But what it means, where it will take you, what it will cost, I have no idea.

"To be honest, my son, I have put all of those things out of my mind. I haven't thought on Bethlehem, or your first Passover, or on any of the other strange and wonderful events of your child-hood in years and years. Sometimes they seem like a dream to me—until I stumble again upon the coin I was given by the magi. Or until you say something like you did today."

"No one could have done more to—" but I was interrupted by Judas and Simon arguing in the dark.

"Mother, Simon has my cloak!"

"Do not!"

We ate breakfast in uneasy, uncomfortable silence. Just before I left, Mary made me promise that I would be in Cana in a cou-ple of weeks for the wedding of the daughter of one of her best friends. I promised I would.

And when breakfast was completed, I hugged them all and took off heading south for the wilderness where I heard that John the Baptist was preaching.

The call had come. The time had come to answer it.

REPORTS OF JOHN THE BAPTIST

But less than a mile from home, as dawn was breaking, it didn't seem like such a good idea.

I mean, I still didn't know what I was supposed to *do*. Everything I'd heard in the synagogue, everything I'd studied in Nazareth, everything I'd learned in every Aramaic and Greek parchment I could get my hands on, all led to this—but what was it?

I knew I wanted to teach. I knew I wanted to share God's love. That much was clear. It was just all of the details in between that were fuzzy.

As the sun rose higher in the sky, I began to see my fellow travelers. I passed a large caravan of traders headed for Tyre. I saw farmers walking slowly to the market in Nazareth. At one point I overtook a troop of Roman soldiers. They were marching smartly and their armor glittered in the sun. As I passed the individual men, I was startled to see how few looked like the Romans or their mercenaries I had grown accustomed to in Galilee. These men were giants, with flaming red hair or hair the color of ripe wheat. They spoke an unknown, but melodious language. It was obvious that they had been marching for many days. I figured them for volunteers or perhaps conscripts from the wild, fierce lands of Gaul where even the Roman armies feared to tread.

That night, I gratefully accepted an invitation to join a large campfire of fellow travelers. Most were Greeks. I shared a loaf with a man who was quoting from the Greek poets Meleager and Philodemus—both of whom were born in Galilee.

After my prayers that night, I stared at the sky. Stars waxed and waned as clouds began to move in from the Great Sea to the west.

What does this all mean? With each step, I somehow feel I am closer to understanding this strange clarion call that I feel in my soul. And why do I have this feeling that John's life and mine are so intertwined?

That hundreds have responded to his unflinching call to repentance means he has touched a nerve with our people. I hear he even has followers. But how long will he be allowed to speak?

Thoughts like these and a thousand more besides darted about in my head until sleep washed them all away.

BAPTIZED BY JOHN

The rest of my journey to Bethabara was uneventful. On the last day, I was joined by a handful of Pharisees and Sadducees who, of course, would neither speak to me nor even acknowledge me. Although these were the two dominant religious orders of our day, I had never actually seen a Sadducee, since most are found in and around Jerusalem. The Pharisees were everywhere and were supposedly the eyes and ears of the Herodians. We had all been warned to watch our tongues around the Pharisees. But why these unlikely co-travelers were heading to hear the words of John the Baptist was beyond me—unless they desired a public show of their famed "humility" through his baptism.

Finding John was easy—it seemed that everybody in this wild and rugged part of Judea had either already heard him or was en route to hearing him! I just followed the crowds down the sloping roads toward Bethabara.

At last I came to a crowd of people sitting on the banks of the muddy Jordan. John had apparently found a place that looked like a natural amphitheater, with the water as the stage. I squeezed into the back row, straining to see and hear him, as he stood thigh-deep in the water below. Overhead, the sky continued to darken as more clouds tumbled in from the west.

It was one of the defining moments of my life.

John was gaunt to the point of emaciation, his hair long and unruly, his voice a croaking rasp from nonstop preaching.

But his words! His words!

". . . again I say, repent! Repent! The kingdom of heaven is at hand! Make ready the way of the Lord, make his paths straight. Every valley shall be filled, every mountain and hill shall be flattened. The crooked shall become straight, the rough ways pounded smooth. And only then shall *all* flesh see the salvation of God!"

I was mesmerized. I could feel my heart speeding up. I inched forward, hoping not to miss a single word. I felt that my whole life had been shaped for this very moment.

Suddenly, John pointed my way. I thought he was pointing at me and my heart skipped a beat. But he was indicating the Sadducees and Pharisees who had arrived about the same time I had. With their fine clothes and haughty manners, they were painfully obvious in this crowd of farmers, fishermen, and soldiers.

"Oh, you offspring of snakes!" John roared, staring directly at them. "Who warned you to flee from the wrath to come? Don't come here for a show, come because you genuinely repent of your ways. Show the fruit of your repentance. You're not immune because you can trace your ancestry right back to Abraham. The time is coming when the axe will lay into the trees of your barren lives and you will be cast into the consuming flames."

The words first troubled, then thrilled me. My head was spinning. I felt like I was on the verge of something miraculous.

John's words also struck one young Pharisee like a slap to the face. He tumbled down through the crowd, mindless of the bodies before him, and flung himself at John's feet in the water. He was joined by several others, including a grizzled, veteran soldier.

"What then shall I do?" the Pharisee cried.

John stared for a moment at the men cowering in the water, then his stern face softened.

"If you have two coats, give one to someone who has none. And if you have food, give half to the hungry."

A second man, apparently a tax collector, said, "What shall I do, Master?"

John said, "Don't collect any more than what is appointed to you."

And then the soldier raised his head. "And I, Master? What must I do?"

John stared evenly at the man. "You must never again extort money or accuse innocent people falsely. Be content with your wages."

I could see the young men shaking and shivering, though the day was already warm despite the heavy cloud cover. Then I noticed I was trembling as well.

One of the other soldiers shouted, "Surely this man is the long-promised Messiah!" Others took up the shout.

Suddenly, the remaining Pharisees and Sadducees stormed down from the cliffs, their faces twisted with rage. They carefully stood on the banks of the river and pointed at John.

"Are you the Christ?" they demanded.

"No, I am not the Christ."

"Then who are you, little man? Are you Elijah?"

John smiled. "I am not."

"Are you the Prophet?"

"No."

The angry men conferred a moment before the eldest addressed John, again in a voice loud enough for those at the back of the crowd—like me—to hear.

"Then who are you? Give us a straight answer to take back to those who sent us. What do you say about yourself?"

John held firm and answered them by quoting Isaiah: "I am the voice of one calling in the desert, 'Make straight the way of the Lord.'"

"But why do you baptize in water if you are not the Christ, nor Elijah, nor the Prophet?" the eldest Pharisee asked with a sneer.

"I baptize you with the water of repentance, but I'm telling you that one stands among you now who will come after me, one who is more powerful than I, whose sandals I am not fit to carry. He will baptize you with the Holy Spirit and with fire. His winnowing fork is in his hand and he will clear his threshing floor, gathering his wheat into the barn and burning up the chaff with an unquenchable fire!"

Then it happened.

I found myself walking/falling/stumbling forward toward John, his words ringing in my ears like a mighty roar.

When John saw me, his face split in a smile and he opened his arms wide. The densely packed listeners pulled away before me, opening a path to the river. Even the indignant Pharisees and Sadducees stepped aside.

The roaring grew louder and louder and was changing into some kind of celestial song. The louder it grew, the more strains I heard, the more words I understood.

We embraced. Tears streamed down both of our faces. I fell to my knees.

I was barely able to choke out, "John, my friend, baptize me."

But John sank down in front of me and said, "No. I see now that I need to be baptized by you, not the other way around."

The way was clear. Or rather, it was clearing. I saw what I needed to do. The roar in my brain was now a full choir of angelic voices, singing and praising God's name.

I said, "Please John, let it be so now. It is proper for us to do this in this manner in order to fulfill all righteousness."

After a heartbeat, John nodded.

He gently cupped my head in his hands and immersed me.

It was as if a bolt of lightning struck me! Behind my closed eyes in the murky water, untold faces flashed before me, faces of all ages, all races, all times.

I knew!

I knew my call, my mission! I was to spread the Good News to all people for all time. I was to continue John's work of repentance, but adding the awful wonderful incomprehensible element of the God of the Universe's all-encompassing love.

I was His Son.

This was our message.

I remembered Bethlehem as if I were an active participant, not a mere babe in arms.

I saw distant lands. I saw more faces. I saw demons and angels. I saw three rough Roman crosses on a nameless hill.

I saw all of this and more in the heartbeat that John held me beneath the water.

And when I came up, the music that was inside me seemed to fill the air.

Above us, the oily black clouds suddenly scrolled back and the sun shone directly above us. I stared into it, but the light didn't hurt or blind.

And a flash of light, brighter still than the sun, only soothing and empowering, separated from the heavens and hurled toward me. For a moment, it took the shape of a dove, then it enveloped me.

Out of the corner of my eye, I saw John staring heavenward, his mouth agape in wonder.

And then a voice filled the air around us. All of those assembled on the banks looked frantically about in every direction to see its source.

But I knew it came from my Father above.

The voice said, "*This is my Son, whom I love, and with whom I am well pleased.*"

I was filled with a strength and a power I had never known.

I was filled with a vision, a quest, a message of a clarity I had never known.

It had begun.

TEMPTATION IN THE WILDERNESS

I left in a daze, retreated into the wilderness, seeking to understand the full scope of what the Lord had laid on my heart.

I knew that the Word dwelt inside me. Was I worthy of it? And what about the horrific, demonic images I saw? What did they mean? I needed time. I needed some isolation to think and pray.

I stumbled around the desert for days, often forgetting to eat or drink, lost in prayer and thought. I slept during the heat of the day, then emerged in the cool of the evening, assembling, assimilating, sorting all that I had seen and heard and felt.

In time, I came upon a shepherd—at least he was dressed like a shepherd. He was sitting alone on a boulder playing a flute beneath a fat, full moon. The music was strange and seductive, sickly sweet and slightly nauseating.

What kind of sheep are soothed by such sensuous music? I wondered.

When I rounded the boulder, I saw. There were no sheep, only row after row of snakes, vipers, and poisonous serpents, all methodically bowing in the shepherd's direction in the light of the moon. I automatically recoiled and glanced at the shepherd.

He never turned from his task.

"Greetings, Jesus of Nazareth, the so-called king of the Jews, the Christ," he said, his voice as sweet as honey.

His tune finished, the strange shepherd clapped his hands and the hundreds of snakes disappeared silently into the night.

Then he turned to me.

"I was wondering when you would show up."

Even in the moonlight, I could see the shepherd was a young man of extraordinary beauty. He looked like the statues of the Greek gods in Tyre and Sepphoris. He was amazingly handsome.

But he was not a shepherd.

He was Satan.

And when he smiled, his teeth were rotten and his breath stank. Somewhere, a jackal cried in pain.

"But I have been a negligent host. You must be hungry, Jesus of Nazareth. Alas, this far from civilization there is precious little bread. I don't require food. But you do."

For the first time, I noticed the gnawing sensation in my stomach. How long had it been since I had eaten last? A day? A week? Two weeks? I could scarcely remember when I had last had a drink of water, either.

Somehow the moonlight suddenly seemed lighter and the entire landscape around us was bathed in a weird, orange glow.

The shepherd bounded off the boulder to a large pile of stones. I had seen these stones before throughout the desert, but I had never noticed until this moment how much they looked like loaves of freshly baked bread. My mouth watered involuntarily.

"Ah, what have we here, O Son of Man? Feel that power surging in your veins? You have the power to turn these stones into bread to feed yourself. And more, you have the power to turn *all* of these stones into bread. You know it is true. The Romans distribute free bread all the time to promote Caesar's kingdom. How much more you could do. Jesus, you could feed the world! Imagine: no more hunger, no more pain, no more beggars lying like living skeletons in the street—and all because of you. Surely you wouldn't be so selfish as to keep such an awesome power to yourself?"

Satan held two loaves in front of me.

He's good, I thought, *not that I expected any less from the Prince of Darkness. But our physical needs must always defer to our spiritual ones.*

"Man shall not live by bread alone," I said firmly, even as my stomach growled in protest, "but by every word that proceedeth out of the mouth of God."

Satan merely shrugged and tossed the stones over his shoulder.

"T'would appear that I have misjudged you, Jesus. Forgive me. It was an unworthy effort on my part.

"Now to the real business at hand. You have been given a mandate by your Father. You have a wonderful message to spread to the nations. Your holy task is to spread that message to as many people as quickly as possible.

"Well, Jesus of Nazareth, you've picked the perfect time to accomplish your mission. A Roman peace pervades the known world. Fine roads connect the smallest, most insignificant village to Roman civilization. Either Greek or Roman is spoken by even the meanest leper. Since the dawn of man, there has never been a better time to spread this Word of yours!"

Satan stood dramatically in front of me, his arms akimbo, his beautiful face pensive as if he were pondering life's greatest mysteries.

"But suppose, just suppose, dear Jesus, what if these glorious words of yours were—perish the thought—ignored? What if instead of creating love, they create hostility or outright hatred? You've seen what the Pharisees and Sadducees are doing with John. How much more will your words be shouted down? What if you spoke and no one listened to a carpenter from Nazareth?"

He was in my face now, his great reeking breath choking me.

"What if those who live in the darkness, after hearing your marvelous words of love, actually *prefer* to stay in the darkness? People are like that, Jesus of Nazareth—believe me, I know. Words are nice, but what these earthlings want are deeds! Miracles! The showier the better."

He walked in excited circles, rubbing his smooth face, lost in thought.

"That's it! We need a miracle! A miracle that will convert all of Judea in one fell swoop! Something they'll talk about for generations! Hang on!"

And with that, Satan grabbed my arm.

The sky went black for a moment and I felt a blast of cold air on my face. When I opened my eyes, we were standing atop the tallest pinnacle of the great tower of the Temple in Jerusalem!

"Picture this," Satan said, his voice tinged with genuine excitement. "At high noon on the Sabbath, in front of the assembled multitudes—and trust me, I can raise a crowd in a hurry!—you'll step off this very tower!

"Of course, you and I know your Heavenly Father will send his angels to catch you and carry you gently to earth. But what a sensation that will cause! I'm telling you Nazarene, even Caiaphas himself will come around to your side after that! You'll convert them all. Then you can turn your attention to the Gentiles—even to Rome herself. That's what your Father wants, isn't it? Why waste time? Save them all while you can."

I stood on the edge of the tower and looked at Jerusalem sleeping below me.

Ah, Jerusalem, there will be others who will take Satan up on his offer—and you will pay the bloody price time and time again.

No, I have a relationship with my Father. My Father's care for me extends to all of his creation, even to the tiny sparrows sleeping at my feet. I'll not be tempted to exploit that unsurpassed love or put my God to the test, no matter how easy Satan's way may appear to be.

I looked at him standing expectantly by my side.

"You shall not tempt the Lord thy God," I said.

The sky went black again and this time the wind was colder and sharper. When I opened my eyes, we were standing somewhere above the Earth on an impossibly tall mountain. I could somehow see the lights of all of the nations of the world.

Satan was no longer dressed like a shepherd. Now he towered above the mountain, dressed like a conquering emperor, resplendent in bright steel and crimson silks. His face filled the heavens, his voice boomed over every hill and valley.

"Jesus, listen to me. You know that I am the Prince of this world. It was given to me when I was…when I *left* your Father's side. I own it!

"But your wise answers and compassion have shown me that only you are worthy to rule the world's kingdoms. Where I dabble in men's affairs, pleasing myself with petty cruelties and senseless invasions, you would be a great and wondrous king, a righteous king, the kind of king these mortals deserve.

"And so, I give them to you."

With a great flourish, the dark turned to daylight and I could see every civilization on Earth.

"They're yours to command—and save," Satan sang. "Just bow down and worship me. One time, that's all.

"Think of the good you'll do. Instead of chaos and wars and starvation, you'll lead this miserable little dustball into a golden age of peace and prosperity.

"Fail them now, and in a few short years your followers will be massacring each other in your name. Men will enslave others in your name. There will be mass slaughter and mass starvation. And you can stop it now for all time with a single word."

Satan is right, of course. He always uses truth as a starting point. That's why he is so dangerous. His choices are rarely between good and evil. They are more often the difference between a good and a lesser good.

To choose his way, the easy way, would be a lesser good.

It would not be my Father's way.

And that is always the way that I must choose. No matter the cost.

"Away with you, Satan!" I said wearily. "For it is written, 'You shall worship the Lord your God, and him only you shall serve.'"

The giant face laughed carelessly and vanished.

I felt my strength ebbing. I was painfully weak and tired.

Suddenly, I was surrounded by gentle, loving faces.

Angels!

In their tender ministrations, I closed my eyes.

THE LAMB OF GOD

When I awoke, the sun was breaking in the east.

I was still weak, but I was alive.

How long had I been alone? It seemed like more than a month.

But in that time, I had come to understand more of who I was and what was required of me.

I brushed myself off and began, somewhat unsteadily, heading back toward the Jordan. Back to John.

Back to the world that had been waiting for the message I was bringing since the dawn of time.

When I finally emerged from the desert near Bethabara, I was gaunt and haggard—but reinvigorated. John was still preaching and the crowds were still surging to hear him. I tried to be inconspicuous, sitting near the back of the crowd while I continued to sort out what it had all meant.

No such luck.

John again pointed at me, smiling, and said: "Look, the Lamb of God, who takes away the sin of the world! *This* is the man I talked about when I said, 'A man who comes after me has surpassed me because he was before me.' I myself did not know him, but the reason I came baptizing with water was that he might be revealed to Israel."

I shifted uncomfortably on the hard ground. Everyone was looking at me. John kept speaking, his voice rising in intensity.

"I saw the Spirit come down from heaven like a dove and remain on him. I would not have known him, except that the one who sent me to baptize with water told me: 'The man on whom you see the Spirit come down and remain is he who will baptize with the Holy Spirit.'

"My friends, I have seen. And I testify that *this* is the Son of God!"

Later, I came down to the riverside to pay my respects to John. His teaching, his call, were the most inspired I had ever heard in my life. I owed him much.

He was talking with some of his followers, with his back to me. When he saw them looking wide-eyed at me, he turned to greet me as well.

"Behold the Lamb of God," he said again.

With that, two of his disciples left John's side and stood respectfully behind me and remained there as I hugged John and thanked him. When I left, they followed me.

I said, "Uh, gentlemen, what do you want?"

The smaller man answered, "Rabbi (which means teacher), where are you staying?"

I said, "Not far, but...you're welcome to join me."

And so they did, and we spent the rest of the day talking and in prayer. One of the men eventually left to return to John. But the smaller man, called Andrew, remained. That night, Andrew disappeared, but rejoined me just as I was preparing for bed.

"Jesus," Andrew said, "this is my brother, Simon Peter. I told him that you are the Messiah."

Simon Peter came bounding up, a robust, ruddy-faced man with the powerful arms of a lifelong fisherman. His grip was like steel.

"It is good to meet you, Simon," I said. "You will be called Cephas (which, when translated, means *Peter*)."

NATHANAEL AND PHILIP

The next morning, to fulfill my last promise to my mother, we left for the wedding in Cana. At first, it felt strange to have Andrew and Simon Peter traveling with me, asking me questions. But if I were to teach, then I needed someone to teach!

Along the way we passed another man. They called him Philip. Like Andrew and Peter, he was from Bethsaida, and they all knew each other. He fell in with us for a short while. It seemed like a perfect fit. After a few minutes, I said, "Philip, follow me."

And he did.

Later that morning, Philip left us to find a friend. Philip later told us that when he found Nathanael (or, as the Greeks called him, Bartholomew), he said, "Hey! We have found the one Moses wrote about in the Law, and about whom the prophets also wrote! His name is Jesus of Nazareth, the son of Joseph."

And, according to Philip, Nathanael laughed and said, "Nazareth! Can anything good come out of Nazareth?"

Philip just shrugged and invited him to come along.

A little while later, we spotted the two of them coming up the road.

I turned to Andrew and Peter and said loud enough for them to hear me, "Now, *here* is a true Israelite! There's nothing false about this man!"

Nathanael cocked an eyebrow and said, "How do you know me?"

Without thinking, I said, "I saw you while you were still under the fig tree before Philip called you."

And suddenly, I realized I had done exactly that! It was as natural and as effortless as breathing. What else was there to learn about this call I had received?

Nathanael looked stunned. "Rabbi, you *are* the Son of God. You *are* the king of Israel."

"Nathanael, you believe because I told you I saw you under the fig tree. You shall see greater things than that."

And again, I suddenly knew it was true—and more!

I said, "Truly I tell you, you shall see heaven open and the angels of God ascending on the Son of Man!"

The five of us walked in silence after that as I digested what was happening, what *had* happened, to me.

It seems that with this great call comes great power. And, I suspect, great responsibility.

But over the course of the next few days, the incident was not mentioned again. And by the time we neared Cana, we were all fast friends, laughing and talking and praying together long into the night.

THE WEDDING AT CANA

I always enjoy visiting Cana, passing the great stands of olive trees and the vast fields of wheat in the lush Esdraelon valley.

Along with Nain and Cana, my little village of Nazareth has the only significant Hebrew population in all of Lower Galilee.

As we walked, Andrew remarked that the three villages were like islands amid a sea of Gentiles, small outcroppings of tradition and faith. At the same time, while I was growing up, it enabled me to meet men and women of other traditions, other faiths. It had been a valuable education.

As we paused for a drink by a well just outside Cana, Andrew asked me, "Jesus, do you know the young couple?"

"Barely," I answered. "Their parents are friends of my mother's— but it was important to her that I attend. And knowing my mother, she would insist that the four of you come along. The more the merrier!"

"Very thoughtful," Andrew said. "I'm never too busy to attend a wedding."

"Oh, it isn't weddings themselves that you like, Andrew," Simon Peter snickered. "It's the week of feasting and dancing that follows!"

Andrew sighed. "If only my parents had given you away at birth as they'd originally planned, Peter. I *knew* they'd made a mistake in keeping you."

By the time we arrived, the wedding celebration was into its third day. I sought out Mary and she cried as if I had been gone at sea for a year. We talked briefly. I think she sensed something was different about me after my time with John, but there was no time to fill her in.

We paid our respects to the lovely Jael and her handsome husband Besai. Besai told me he'd worked for Jael's father for a year as compensation for her hand in marriage. Then he'd built a snug room for the two of them in his father's house.

"She is a rare beauty, Besai," I said. "I suppose you've happened to notice how her eyes flash and how her hair reflects the sun when she walks."

"Oh yes," Besai said dreamily. "And Jesus, you will be happy to know that, over the past couple of days, Jael has been spending long hours talking with Mary, your mother."

Even though my mother had never remarried after Joseph died, young girls often sought her out for encouragement and insight. Children and young people had always loved her.

"It is obvious that the two have forged some kind of bond, despite the difference in their ages," I said.

"I'm nearly fourteen and Jael has been thirteen for several months," Besai protested, "but she is very mature for her age."

"I have no doubt. Perhaps my mother sees something of herself as a young girl in your Jael."

"If that is so, then I am truly blessed," Besai said courteously, then excused himself to attend to his other guests.

After he was gone, I prayed under my breath: *Father, please bless this union.*

It wasn't long before Besai and Peter were laughing and dancing to the happy, rhythm-heavy wedding music. Apparently, Peter made friends—and enemies—easily.

So I found myself a quiet couch in a corner room, accompanied only by a bowl of the glorious grapes that grow so readily around Cana, and leaned back to watch the festivities. Like Andrew, I love weddings. I've always thought they were one of my Father's greatest inventions! And while it is only a pale imitation of the love my Father has for his people, seeing a young couple so in love reminds me of the home I've left behind.

Suddenly, my mother appeared beside me, a worried look on her lovely face.

"What is wrong, mother? Surely Jael has not told you some deep, dark secret that threatens this blessed event."

I was teasing, but mother was in no mood to joke.

"Jesus, there has been a terrible mistake. Someone has badly misjudged the amount of wine needed for the week. The family's stocks are almost depleted and there are still four days of feasts to go!"

Mary chewed on her lip. I could tell she was summoning her courage to ask me a hard question, or perhaps make a difficult request. I steeled myself.

"Jesus, if they run out of wine, the party is ruined. Jael and Besai will be crushed. Their reputations will be tarnished—and this wasn't even their fault!"

I peered at her evenly. I knew where this conversation was going.

"Son," she said quietly, "can you do something about it?"

I must have flinched slightly, because she put her hand on my arm. Did she somehow know something must have happened with me in the River Jordan?

Or was she simply asking me to go buy more wine? Surely she must know I had left her all of my earnings. And where would I buy more at this hour?

But something else was happening within me. I felt the power that our Father in heaven had given me surge within my body. I somehow knew that, with God's help, I had the power to miraculously make a change, to please my mother, to save the wedding party.

I also somehow knew that once I began to use that God-given power, my brief time of transition and reflection would be over. The real work would begin.

So soon? Must it begin so soon? I thought sadly. *Once we step on this road, there can be no turning back.*

And in that moment, I had another terrible vision, but it was like the continuation of what I had seen in the river. This time I saw thousands of people screaming, some crying in pain, others in jubilation. I saw the cruel sneers of Roman officials and heard dark plots whispered in shadowy corners. I saw another dizzying array of faces, Jew and Gentile alike. I saw armies clashing and refugees fleeing, and lost children whimpering amid the colonnade of the Temple. I saw Satan, first a shepherd, then a soldier, then a priest, laughing.

And, at last, I saw the same three makeshift crosses I had seen before, sitting atop a windswept hill on a raw, blustery evening.

It was as though I was floating above the crosses, looking down on the scene below. And, at the foot of the central cross, a single woman lay prostrate, weeping uncontrollably, as black drops of blood spattered her in a hot rain.

My blood.

All for a little wine.

"Mother, my dear mother, why do you involve me?" I whispered. "My time has not yet come."

But she knew that I could not refuse her, anymore than I could refuse anyone who asked something of me in faith. Perhaps wishing for a few more days of peace was selfish after all.

She smiled at me, mistaking my hesitation for shyness. Then she turned and addressed the servants who had remained a respectful distance away, awaiting her orders.

"Do whatever he tells you," she said firmly.

They looked at me with expectant eyes. I forced a smile.

Nearby stood six stone water jars, the kind used for ceremonial washing. Because Besai's family was obviously wealthy, these were uncommonly large, each holding perhaps twenty to thirty gallons.

"Please fill these jars with water, then leave them here," I said. The servants quickly obeyed.

I looked around for Mary, but she'd discreetly moved away as well, blending into the crowd in the banqueting room.

And when I was alone with the six stone jars, I prayed that my Father would allow me to turn them to wine. Not for me, not even for Mary, but for Besai and the shiny-eyed Jael.

Father, if this is to be the second watershed moment of my life for you, I prayed, *then let these dear young people celebrate it in style so that they may begin their life journey together without a hint of sadness.*

When I opened my eyes, I could see the servants still hovering in the doorway, fidgeting from one foot to the other, glancing at each other anxiously. They looked like deer surprised at night by a torch. It was plain that it was one of them that had erred in ordering the wine. And from the panicked look of the eldest servant and the sweat that drenched his tunic, it was easy to spot the guilty party.

I motioned to him.

"Draw some out and take it to the master of the banquet in the great hall where the feast continues."

The old fellow eyed me suspiciously, but he nervously did what I said. He spilled half before he ever reached the head table. The other servants followed a safe distance behind.

The master of the banquet paused in mid-speech and sipped the wine. Then he noisily drained the cup and ordered more, a giant smile spreading across his face.

When all of the wedding guests had been served, the banquet master offered a toast:

"Everyone usually brings out the choice wine first—and *then* brings out the cheaper stuff after most of the guests have had too much to drink!"

The guests erupted in spontaneous cheers, banging their cups, crying for more. The banquet master shouted for quiet and wrapped his arm around Besai's neck.

"But Besai here has saved the best for last. This is *incredible* wine!"

The place went crazy and the servants worked furiously keeping the cups filled.

But each time they passed my corner room, they gave me the most curious looks: apologetic, appreciative, and even a little bit frightened—all rolled into one.

In time, Nathanael plopped down beside me.

"Master, the old servant told us what you did. You told me I'd see great wonders—but I didn't know they'd begin so soon!"

Oh Nathanael, there's so much yet to see, I thought sadly. *If only it would all be as easy and happy as this.*

Just then, Jael, her dark eyes glowing, glided up, as light as a gazelle.

"And *you*, Jesus of Nazareth, you owe me this dance!"

I tried to protest, but Nathanael shoved me roughly to my feet. Jael gaily took my hand and we joined the circle of dancers.

Faster and faster we danced, to a tune that was ancient when Father Abraham was young. We passed the flutes and harps, and amid the timbrels there was Simon Peter, bashing merrily away.

And on the far side of the circle, alone against the wall, stood my mother. She smiled proudly and waved as we passed. I'm not sure she even knew what had happened, only that I had somehow made things right.

I smiled back.

And so it has begun, I prayed silently. *Dear Father, give me the strength and wisdom to see it through. Find me worthy.*

But meanwhile, Jael must have seen my pensive look. She playfully gave my arm a jerk, and I resumed singing to the music.

Thankfully, Besai soon cut in and took my place. I retired back to my favorite corner, and the dancing and singing continued long into the night, ringing over the hills surrounding sleepy Cana.

John Taken Prisoner

The following day, the five of us left for Capernaum with my mother. I felt a distant tugging to return to the Sea of Galilee.

We hadn't gone long before we encountered a group of Jews talking excitedly under a Roman bridge.

"God's peace on you, brothers," I said as we approached. "What news do you have?"

"Oh, it is terrible news indeed," a merchant answered. "Herod has imprisoned John!"

"It is for preaching that Herod sinned in marrying Philip's wife Herodias!" another said.

John? In prison? I fear the worst for him. Father, strengthen and empower him. Soften Herod's heart to him.

"Where now, Rabbi?" Nathanael said gingerly, still holding his throbbing head.

"Still toward the northern shore of the Sea of Galilee," I said absently.

May God's love be with you, dear John.

One ministry had ended.

My own had just begun.

CHAPTER TWO

Gathering Disciples

NICODEMUS

I lost myself in Capernaum's busy market, teeming with farmers and fisherfolk and the wide-eyed young soldiers who comprised the large Roman garrison. I spent several days there, making friends and regaining my strength. I had long talks with my mother, walking along the beautiful shore of the Sea of Galilee. But I must confess that I'm not sure she ever understood what I was doing—or why. Eventually, Andrew and Peter needed to tie up some loose ends with their successful fishing business. They left with my blessing.

There was one more thing I needed to do before I felt empowered to begin my new ministry. I felt that I must go to Jerusalem to celebrate the upcoming Passover.

We returned via Cana, where Mary met my brothers and went home to Nazareth. Then Nathanael, Philip, and I continued to Jerusalem.

Once in the city, we were surprised to discover that word of what John had said about me had spread, at least among his disciples. A few people even knew about the incident with the wine at the wedding in Cana! A number of hurting people came to me, begging for relief. Through prayer and my Father's help, I was able to heal them. But I asked them to keep their healings quiet. The Romans were edgy and weren't in the mood for an uprising, popular or otherwise! Too many "messiahs" had already died in recent years leading various abortive revolts and rebellions.

After a few nights, a Pharisee named Nicodemus came to see me at the inn where we were staying. The fact that a Pharisee was at my door didn't surprise me. Some of them were receptive to my teaching and I often dined with them. Nevertheless, I had already realized that they were going to be a source of much frustration. As a group, they were so close to the truth, and I had to admire the way they tried to protect the poor from the greed of the Sadducees (that was why they said that the law was for *all* to obey, not just for some—to gain for all the protection of the law). But too many of them had lost sight of their ultimate goal and began to see the law itself as the ultimate good and themselves as superior to others. Even the sages said that there were seven kinds of Pharisees and five of them were hypocrites. Besides, they were now part of the establishment themselves and so were too afraid of any changes. Most of them had become much too cozy with the Romans for my taste.

What surprised me was that a Pharisee of such stature as Nicodemus should come to see me. He was a member of the inner circle of leaders, a group that had already denounced what I was doing and saying on several occasions. I had no doubt that few of Nicodemus's friends would have been happy to know of his presence in my small room that night.

He said, "Rabbi, I know you are a teacher who has come from God—for no one else could perform the miraculous signs you are doing if God *wasn't* on your side!"

"Thank you," I said, "but there is more to my message than signs. Truly, I tell you that no one—not even a Pharisee—can see the kingdom of God unless he is born again."

Beneath his beautifully oiled and combed beard, Nicodemus broke into a huge frown.

"Uhh, Teacher, how can a man be born again when he is old? I mean, surely he can't reenter his mother's womb, can he?"

I smiled. At least he was trying to understand.

"Truly, Nicodemus, no one can enter the kingdom of God unless he is born of water *and* of the Spirit. My friend, flesh gives birth to flesh, but the Spirit gives birth to spirit.

"You really shouldn't be surprised at me saying 'You must be born again' if you think about it. Listen: the wind blows where it pleases, right? You hear its sound, but you cannot tell where it comes from or where it goes. So it is with everyone who is born of the Spirit."

Poor Nicodemus! He plopped down hard on the floor, his face a study in concentration. "Jesus, how can this be?"

"You are one of Israel's teachers and you do not understand these things?" I said gently. "Truly, Nicodemus, we speak of what we know and we testify to what we have seen with our own eyes. But still your people do not accept our testimony.

"My friend, I have spoken to you of earthly things and yet you do not believe. How then are you going to believe if I speak of heavenly things? No one has ever gone into heaven except the one who came from heaven—the Son of Man. Just as Moses lifted up the snake in the desert, so the Son of Man must be lifted up so that *everyone* who believes in him may have eternal life. Do you follow?"

"I ...I think so," Nicodemus said. "Please, continue."

"Nicodemus, for God so loved the world he gave his one and only Son, that whosoever believes in him will not perish—but have eternal life. You see, God didn't send his Son to condemn the world, but to save it—through him! Whoever believes in him is not condemned, but whoever does not believe in him is already condemned because he has not believed in the name of God's one and only Son.

"Here's what's happened: The light has come into the world, but most men love darkness instead of light because their deeds are evil. You know that everyone who does evil hates light and will avoid lighted places because their evil deeds will be exposed. But whoever lives by the truth comes into the light, so that it may be seen plainly that what he has done has been done through God."

Tears glistened in Nicodemus's eyes.

"Teacher, I choose the light of the Son of Man—here and now, for all times."

We embraced. He warned me that opposition from within the Pharisees was growing dangerously, but that he would do his best to keep the more manic members under control. And then Nicodemus slipped back into the night. I knew I had found a friend for life.

THE SAMARITAN WOMAN

After Passover, we decided to return to Capernaum. I needed some time to rid myself of the disgusting images of money changers and animal salesmen hawking their wares on the beautiful Temple grounds, shouting, blaspheming, bullying, cheating the faithful.

Instead of taking the long way around on the east side of the Jordan, we walked *through* Samaria. During our stay in Jerusalem, I'd heard many people reviling the Samaritans, calling them filthy half-breeds, scum of the earth, and other names too cruel to repeat. Nathanael and Philip, of course, were shocked and tried to talk me out of it. But these were God's children, no matter what they were alleged to have done—or to have not done—in the past. They—no less than the Jews—needed to hear of God's love.

So off we went, due north. Besides, I was anxious to see what kind of "monsters" they really were!

Not surprisingly, the trip was quiet and pleasant. The few people we passed on the road looked like people I had seen everywhere—normal, God-fearing, humble, hardworking folk. Of course, most jumped when I greeted them—they weren't used to strange men with Galilean accents speaking kindly to them!

About noon we came upon the town of Sychar, near the famed plot of ground that Jacob had given his son Joseph. I had long wanted to see Jacob's Well and, being thirsty, I eagerly sought directions to find it. Nathanael and Philip went on into town to find dinner.

As I sat by the ancient well, a beautiful young Samaritan woman approached. She carried a heavy clay urn to draw water, but I think her main interest was to get a better look at the stranger sitting there—me!

Our eyes met and I smiled. "Please, would you give me a drink?"

Like the others, she flinched when she heard my Galilean accent. She took a step backward and her body tensed for the standard verbal assault.

"How...how is it that you, a Jew, ask me for a drink?" she stammered. "Your people have no dealings with Samaritans."

Her answer saddened me. She was, of course, right. Of all the peoples of the world, the Jews most despised the Samaritans, and they suffered much at our hands.

"Young lady, if you but knew of the gift of God, and who it is asking you for a drink, you would have asked him for a drink of the living water instead." I deliberately used a slang term for running water, which I intended to give a new meaning.

Naturally, she looked puzzled, but her body posture relaxed slightly.

"Uh, sir, you have nothing to draw with and this well is very deep. Where then are you going to get this 'living water' you're talking about?"

Father, forgive us for what we're doing to these gentle people.

I motioned to the well.

"Whoever drinks of this water will thirst again. But whoever drinks of the water that I shall give them will have a fountain of water springing up—springing up into everlasting life!"

She placed the heavy urn down and sat on the opposite end of the well, perspiring in the noon sun.

"All right, then, stranger, please give me some of this water you're speaking about, the kind that will take away my thirst forever, the kind that means I won't have to lug this urn out to this well three times a day!"

Her tone was flippant, but I could tell that she was sincerely interested.

"Wonderful!" I said. "Now, go fetch your husband so that he can hear about this living water."

Her lovely face flushed crimson and she stared at her feet.

"I...uh...have no husband."

"I know," I said as kindly as possible. "You don't—you have answered honestly. Instead, you have had five husbands, and the man you're living with now is not your husband, is he?"

The Samaritan woman sprang up from the well and backed away from me, her eyes wide with fear and wonder.

"But...how? How could you..."

Then she fell to her knees.

"Sir, I see now that you are a prophet."

I helped her back to her feet and bid her to sit with me a moment longer. When she was certain I wasn't going to condemn her or preach to her, a torrent of questions tumbled out. Questions she'd been holding inside for years—just waiting for the right opportunity to be asked. And here I was—a prophet—at her well. Apparently, it was too good an opportunity to resist.

"Sir, our fathers worshiped on this mountain. But you Jews say that in Jerusalem alone is the place where one should worship. Well? Which is it?"

A worthy question. This one is bright with promise.

"Young lady, believe me, the time is coming when you will not worship the Father either at this mountain nor in Jerusalem. You're not sure what you worship and we've long said that salvation will solely belong to the Jews. But that coming time is now—when the true believers will worship the Father in spirit and truth. For the Father is seeking believers like that.

"God *is* Spirit, and those who worship him must worship in spirit and truth."

She stared at me for long minutes, her eyes never leaving mine.

"I believe that the Messiah, the only one who will be called the Christ, is coming. And when he comes, he will tell us all things."

I touched her hand lightly. "I am he."

Just then, Philip and Nathanael came bounding up, loaded down with bread and olive oil. I could tell from their faces they were dying to ask me what I was doing talking with a hated Samaritan. Fortunately, they kept their mouths shut. The woman left her waterpot and dashed back into Sychar. We could see her as she encountered other people along the road, talking excitedly, and pointing back toward us.

Nathanael shook his head. "Something's up, Philip. Get ready. I can feel it."

Philip said, "Rabbi, whatever is happening, you still need to eat. Have some of this nice bread."

But I was too busy watching the joyful child of God button-holing total strangers on the road to Sychar.

"I have food to eat of which you do not know, Philip."

Philip peered at Nathanael. "Did someone sneak Jesus food while we were in town?"

I said, "Philip, Nathanael, listen to me: My food is to do the will of him who sent me—and to finish his work.

"Don't you often say, 'There are still four months and *then* comes the harvest?' But I'm telling you, 'Lift up your eyes and look at the fields, man! For they are already ripe for the harvest!' "

Nathanael chewed on his lip, which was his habit when he was trying to follow a new saying.

I continued: "He who reaps the fields I'm talking about receives wages and gathers fruit for eternal life, that both he who sows and he who reaps may rejoice together.

"For in this the old saying is true now more than ever: 'One sows and another reaps.'

"You see, I sent you to reap that for which you have not labored. Others have labored and you have entered into their labors."

By now, a steady stream of Samaritans were quickly heading our way, looking for the man the lovely Samaritan woman was saying had seen her entire life. They crowded around us, peppering me with questions, listening thirstily to my answers.

One thing led to another and when it was all over, we had spent two full days in Sychar, preaching, healing, teaching, listening. During that time, many of the Samaritans believed and were saved.

A delegation of city leaders, including the woman, begged us to stay longer, but our work here was done.

As we were preparing to leave, they stood around us and wished us Godspeed. Then one of the leaders turned to the woman by the well—who had by now left her latest "husband"—and said, "Now we believe, not because of what you said, for now we have heard for ourselves and know that this is indeed the Christ, the Savior of the world."

She blushed again.

THE OFFICIAL'S SON

From Samaria, we made good time back into the more familiar terrain of Galilee.

My first stop was Cana. But we hadn't been in town a few minutes when a royal official came rushing up.

"Good Master," he said, gasping for breath, "my son is dying. Please, I beg you, come with me quickly back to Capernaum!"

I looked evenly at him for a moment as he struggled to catch his breath.

"Unless you see miraculous signs and wonders, you will never believe, will you?"

But the official shook his head vigorously. "Sir, please: All I know is that you must come to Capernaum before my child dies."

This one believes. Though fear originally gave wings to his faith, he now believes.

"You may go," I said. "Your son will live."

He hesitated the barest fraction of a second, then flew out the door to his waiting chariot.

We followed toward Capernaum a few hours later. A couple of days following, the official sent word back to us that he was met by his servants on the road to Capernaum. The servants told him that his son indeed had recovered. And that it had happened at the hour of our original meeting! His entire family now believed.

REJECTED AT NAZARETH

As before, word of what had happened in Jerusalem and Cana had spread ahead of me and soon we had a long entourage wherever we went in Capernaum. I was invited to speak in a number of synagogues and enjoyed my time telling the Galileans about God's love.

Several old family friends saw me healing a lame man in the market and begged me to return, even for a day, to Nazareth. I had a bad feeling about it, but decided to go anyway.

My family was more confused than anyone about the reports they had been hearing about me. Only Mary kept quiet, but I could see the concern and torment on her face.

Still, I accepted an invitation to read at the synagogue. I asked for the scroll of Isaiah and soon found the passage I was looking for:

"The Spirit of the Lord is on me because he has anointed me to preach good news to the poor. He has sent me to proclaim freedom for the prisoners and recovery of sight for the blind, to release the oppressed, to proclaim the year of the Lord's favor."

I carefully rolled back up the scroll, handed it to the attendant, and looked about the packed synagogue. Every eye was fastened to me.

"Today," I said firmly, "this scripture is fulfilled in your hearing."

There was total silence in the room for several heartbeats. Then, from the back of the room, one of the town's most devout Pharisees said, "Wait a minute! Isn't this Joseph's son?" Soon others were asking that—and similar—questions.

I held my ground.

"I'm sure you will quote this proverb to me: 'Physician, heal yourself! Do here in your hometown what we have heard you've done in Capernaum.'"

There was a general roar of assent. But my Father had not given me this task, this power, to perform miracles on demand, like some court magician.

I said, "Truly, I tell you, no prophet is accepted in his hometown. Did you know that there were many widows in Israel in Elijah's time when the sky was shut for three and a half years and there was famine throughout the land? Yet Elijah was not sent to any of them, but to a widow in Zarephath in the region of Sidon. But there were many others in Israel with leprosy in the time of Elisha the prophet, yet not one of them was cleansed—only Naaman the Syrian."

Well, that cinched it! The synagogue exploded in anger. A mob of men—including many of my former friends—grabbed me and drove me from Nazareth. Philip and particularly Nathanael tried to protect me, scuffling and sometimes fighting with the enraged Nazarenes, but they were soon overwhelmed. Eventually, we found ourselves pushed and beaten to the lip of a steep hill outside town.

The angry men withdrew momentarily, leaving us standing, bloodied and dazed at the edge of the cliff. Then they formed a tight phalanx and rushed us!

They're going to push us to our deaths! Father! Aid us in our need! I prayed desperately.

Brave Philip and Nathanael stepped in front of me, braced their legs, and knotted their fists, waiting for the end.

But it never came.

The men abruptly stopped and began rubbing their faces and heads as if waking from a bad dream.

I grabbed Nathanael and Philip's arms and walked out of Nazareth—right through the midst of the mob. Up the hill

came my mother, running frantically. She had heard the commotion and tried to follow, but some of the women had held
her back.

"Oh, Jesus, I was so worried! They would have killed you!"

I tried to reassure her.

"My time has not yet come, mother. And when it does, it will
be in a place of my Father's choosing. Now, be strong. We must
leave and I fear it will be a long, long time before I ever return to
Nazareth again."

PETER AND ANDREW

We limped toward Capernaum, which was increasingly feeling like home to me. Once there, we rested a couple of
days, then resumed our mission to talk—and listen—to as many
who had ears to hear our message.

My first stop was the Sea of Galilee (or the Lake of Gennesaret
as some called it). It was time to call on a couple of friends.

But once I arrived on the shore, it wasn't long before another
crowd gathered. Never one to pass up an opportunity to share the
good news, I spoke with the people as we walked along the shore-
line. After a while, we came upon the fishing boat I was looking
for—Simon Peter and Andrew's! They were washing their nets
when they saw me and rushed to give me big bear hugs.

With their permission, I climbed into one of their boats and
spoke further with the assembled crowd from a few feet offshore.

When at last I was finished, I grabbed Peter and Andrew.

"Well, boys, how's fishing?"

Peter rolled his eyes. "Rotten. We worked all night and haven't
caught enough to even pay our taxes to that greedy insect
Matthew!"

"Good," I said. "Then let's go fishing! Head on out to deeper water."

"Uh . . . sure. Whatever you say. Andrew: you heard the man— push off!"

We went out a ways until I felt *something* at a certain spot.

"Here. Let down your nets here."

"Only because you say so, Jesus."

And they did as I suggested.

Almost immediately, the boat listed dangerously to the starboard. The nets were nearly jerked from their arms! Andrew screamed for the other two boats to come and help. As they struggled with the load, the others arrived, threw out their nets, and *their* nets were filled to bursting with schools and schools of fish!

When we'd finally managed to haul the silvery cargo aboard, the boats were seriously overweight and began to take on water. Peter struggled across the bloody deck awash in madly thrashing fish and fell to his knees in front of me. "Please leave me, Lord— for I am a sinful man!"

From the nearby boat, two of their partners, who I soon discovered were to be James and John, the sons of Zebedee, did the same.

It was quite a sight—these rough, burly fishermen, kneeling on slippery, waterlogged decks, surrounded by thousands of angry, tail-slapping fish! I shouted to them all: "Don't be afraid! Come, follow me! From now on, I will make you fishers of men."

Then we carefully guided the creaking old boats to shore. John, James, Peter, and Andrew promptly walked away from their boats—leaving their rich haul to be split between their remaining partners—and followed me back into town.

PETER'S MOTHER-IN-LAW

Now there were six. Although a number of people, men and women, were already following me—and sometimes those numbers swelled into the hundreds—in the back of my mind I had the idea for a core group of twelve. As we walked, Nathanael and Philip quickly brought the others up to date on what had happened in recent weeks.

On the outskirts of Capernaum, Peter urged me to come to his home where his mother-in-law, Maariah, was bedridden with one of the many nasty fevers that seemed to breed and thrive in the marshes around the edge of the Sea of Galilee.

Peter and Andrew's joint fishing partnership apparently was quite successful—their house was large and nicely furnished. But Maariah was gravely ill; her skin was hot to the touch. She rolled listlessly in the bed, her eyes shut. As the others stood expectantly around us, I whispered a rebuke of the fever and prayed over her. Immediately, her eyes flew open and her color returned.

"Oh, Simon Peter! Andrew! Why didn't you tell me that we had guests. Here, you poor gentlemen must be starved. Let me see if I can't whip up something in the kitchen. Peter! Where *are* your manners?"

He could only smile helplessly at me.

Within minutes I felt like I'd been a member of this family since birth. Maariah ran a tight household, but was a gracious and loving hostess. She needed to be, for once word of both the fishing expedition and her recovery spread, it seemed that half of Capernaum was forever outside her door, asking for me to come and heal their afflictions.

I tried to accommodate as many suffering people as I could. The most troubling were those possessed by demons. The demons shouted my name when I approached or spewed out the most horrendous profanities and blasphemies. In time, I was forced to deal with the demoniacs far away from Maariah's house, to keep from disrupting the lives of the other families living there.

After a few days, I was exhausted. So, before dawn, I slipped out, looking for a solitary place near the sea to pray and reflect. As comfortable and accepting as Capernaum was, I knew I would need to move on shortly. The people must have sensed it because, before long, they found me, praying alone near the reeds.

An old woman hobbled up and said, "Dear Teacher, pray stay with us forever. There is much good you could do here."

I said, "I must preach the good news of the kingdom of God to the other towns also, because that is why I was sent."

"Then, Master, teach us now," she said. And with that, the woman and the throng around her sat down right there and stared expectantly at me.

So much for a few moment's peace. But thank you Father, for these willing hearts. And so I preached and listened to them until nearly noon.

AN EXORCISM IN THE SYNAGOGUE

On the Sabbath, I was invited to another synagogue. I think Philip and Nathanael were a little wary this time after what had happened in Nazareth, because both sat by the door! Nathanael still had one glorious black eye and wasn't sure he wanted another. But there was no way I could soften or change my message. I again spoke the words my Father had given me.

This time, however, the response was uniformly positive. Those in the synagogue seemed to comprehend what I was trying to say.

Suddenly, the doors of the synagogue flew open. A single man staggered in, covered in filthy rags, his eyes as wild as a captive dove tortured by sadistic children.

"What do you want of us, Jesus—you Nazarene?!" the man roared, his voice strangely hollow. "Have you come to destroy us? Because I know who you are—you are God's holy one!"

The poor man was obviously possessed by a demon, driven to madness by its incessant chatter and sinister whispers in the night. He thrashed about on the floor, pointing at me, and howling incoherently.

Nathanael moved to escort the madman out, but I stopped him.

"Silence, demon!" I shouted. "Get out of him!"

The man—or was it the demon?—shrieked like a woman in birth pains, then was silent. After a heartbeat, the man sat up and looked around, his eyes clear and rational.

"He gives orders with authority even to the foul spirits," I heard one man whisper to another, "and they obey him."

I tried to continue my lesson, but many of the listeners ran out of the synagogue to tell others what they had seen and heard.

A LEPER HEALED

My remaining days in Capernaum were pleasant, if increasingly hectic, as people even from the nearby villages began to stream into town to hear my message or be healed.

One afternoon, I came upon a man afflicted with leprosy. He was a ghastly sight, covered with open sores, his fingers mere nubs, and with most of his nose and ears rotted off. The poor man fell at my feet and croaked, "Lord, if you want to, you can make me clean."

My followers fell back, hissing for the man to leave. But I was filled with compassion for the man's pain and reached forward. I touched his bleeding scalp and whispered to him: "I am willing, my friend. Be clean."

The man collapsed in a heap and transformed before our eyes. His color returned, his sores healed, his extremities grew back. He leaped in the air, shouting with joy.

But I placed a hand on his shoulder. "Please don't tell anyone. Instead, go and show yourself to the priest and offer the sacrifices that Moses commanded for your cleansing as a testimony to them."

"I promise, Master," he said. The man then kissed my hands and dashed away, singing and shouting at the top of his lungs.

Within minutes, a new crowd of people came flooding after us, all buzzing about the healing of the leper. I sighed. The former leper's promise had lasted less than five minutes! So that day ended, as all of them had ended, with me teaching and healing long into the night.

THE PARALYTIC

When I could, generally late at night, I slipped into the lonely places outside of Capernaum to pray and ponder.

After a while, I took my small band of disciples on short trips to the villages of Galilee, continuing to spread the Word. We received lovely, heartfelt receptions virtually everywhere and the crowds continued to flock to us.

Two more men joined our band, Jude, surnamed Thaddaeus, and James, son of Cleophas and Mary. Both were Galileans. To distinguish between the two Jameses, the others took to calling them Big James and Little James. James, the brother of John, was considerably older than James, the son of Alphaeus—so he was Big James. Both Thaddaeus and Little James were quiet, sensitive men, hardworking and shy.

They were with us on one of my forays back into Capernaum after a lengthy visit to the villages northwest of the city. When we returned to Maariah's house, a few children saw us on the

outskirts of town. So, before we'd even had lunch, hundreds had
gathered at her doorstep. Maariah graciously opened her house to
them and dozens crowded inside out of the heat to hear me talk.
Among them, I noticed, were a number of Pharisees.

While I was speaking, four men carried one of their friends on
a stretcher to see me. When they saw that the doors were jammed,
they climbed up on Maariah's roof, found a window, and tied the
pallet with strong ropes. Then they lowered their friend into the
living room where I was sitting and speaking!

Within seconds, everybody stopped listening and began pointing toward the ceiling. When I looked to see what the commotion
was, the poor man was lowered in front of me. He was obviously
paralyzed, his muscles withered and wasted. Though he could not
speak, he implored me to heal him through sunken, hollow eyes.

I looked up at his loyal friends, then back at the man. "Son,
your sins are forgiven," I said.

Immediately, the Pharisees in the room recoiled like they'd been
struck by snakes. "Why does this Nazarene think he can talk like
that?" one said loudly to another. "He's blaspheming! No one can
forgive sins but God!"

Somehow, their dark, twisted thoughts were made known to
me. *These men haven't come to learn, they've come to find an excuse to have me
put away—or killed!*

I said directly to them, "Why are you thinking these things?
Which is easier: to say to a paralytic, 'Your sins are forgiven,' or to
say, 'Get up, take your mat, and walk'?

"Still, so that you'll know that the Son of Man does have the
authority on earth to forgive sins..." I looked again at the paralytic, his eyes now wide with fear, afraid that he *wasn't* going to
get healed, and said, "...I tell you, my brother, 'Get up, take your
mat, and go home.'"

Instantly, his atrophied arms and legs filled out with muscle. The man fell off the mat, carefully pulled himself to his feet, checked his arms and legs, then joyously snaked his way through the closely packed bodies.

Everyone—save one group of Pharisees—broke into spontaneous whistles and cheers, shouting, "We have never seen anything like this!"

MATTHEW

Once again, this healing caused yet more people to stampede toward poor Maariah's house. To save what was left of her furnishings—and larder—I moved again to the open beaches of the Sea of Galilee.

Near where the fishermen brought their catch each day to market, I spotted a single tax collector in his booth, busily at work. His name was Levi, or Matthew, the son of Alphaeus.

When he saw such a large procession coming his way, Matthew jumped up and prepared to flee—thinking, no doubt, that this was a lynching party coming for him, especially when he saw Peter and James at the forefront! And, judging by the looks on their faces, that thought was on more than a few minds.

As Matthew stood there, ready to bolt, I walked up and said, "Follow me."

Matthew rocked on his heels a moment and said, "Sure. Are you hungry?"

So we walked to Matthew's house for lunch. He'd already invited some of his tax collector friends and a few low-level Roman officials, but he bid his servants make room for me and my nine disciples at once. But he didn't include the various Pharisees who had tagged along. They stood outside the door and glared at us, resplendent in their fine clothes and haughty manners.

As we lay around the well-loaded tables, I began to speak to Matthew of the good news.

After a few minutes, the oldest Pharisee couldn't stand it anymore. In voice loud enough for everyone within a block to hear, he asked, "Why does *he* eat with tax collectors and sinners?"

I carefully rose, walked to the doorway, and stood just inches from this pompous, well-perfumed little man. I didn't want there to be any mistake about what I was saying. I said, "It is not the healthy who need a doctor, but the sick. I have not come to call the righteous but the sinners!"

The Pharisees snorted in disgust, wheeled, and paraded away.

I returned to my table, only to have Matthew cry, "Rabbi, let me follow you!"

And so he did. Now we were ten.

BALD PHARISEE AND GOAT-BEARD

In the days that followed, my adversaries among the Pharisees redoubled their efforts to catch me breaking the Law or speaking heresy. Soon I got to know them as well as my own disciples. We even gave them affectionate nicknames. They trailed me around like yapping puppies as I continued to work near Capernaum.

A few days later, I was eating breakfast with my disciples, discussing the schedule for the day, when a couple of my regular Pharisees strolled up.

"John's disciples and the Pharisees are fasting today, Jesus of Nazareth," Bald Pharisee said sweetly. "I don't understand. How come your disciples are *not* fasting?"

I smiled back. "How can the guests of the bridegroom fast while he is with them? They can't! But the time will come when the bridegroom will be taken from them and on that day, they will fast."

The man that Nathanael had dubbed "Goat-beard" snorted and began to retort, but thought better of it.

"No one sews a patch of unshrunk cloth on an old garment," I continued. "If he does, the new piece will pull away from the old one, making the tear ever worse, right?

"Likewise, no one pours new wine into old wineskins. If he does, the wine will burst the skins and both the wine and wineskins will be forever ruined. No, you pour new wine into new wineskins."

Goat-beard and Bald Pharisee looked at each other, then departed without another word.

Later that week we traveled to Nain, and on the Sabbath we went to the synagogue there. My Pharisee entourage passed us, heading for their usual places of honor. Almost immediately, a man with a shriveled hand walked meekly up and begged me to heal him.

The Pharisees and their friends sat like vultures, waiting for me to act.

I said, "Stand up in front of everyone."

Confused and frightened by the attention, the man nevertheless did just that.

Then I asked the people in the synagogue, "Which is lawful on the Sabbath? To do good or to do evil? To save a life—or to kill?"

No one responded. Goat-beard's whole face was twitching now.

They didn't care about this poor man with his pitiful claw of a hand. They only wanted to be proven right. Someone else's suffering meant nothing to them.

How much these Pharisees have to learn—and unlearn, I thought sadly.

Finally, I told the man, "Stretch out your hand."

He tentatively complied. And when he did, his hand was completely restored.

Nearly incoherent with anger, the Pharisees and Herodians stormed out of the synagogue—to plot, I had no doubt, my death.

After the service, my ten disciples huddled around me.

"What now, Jesus?" Philip asked.

"Maybe we should give those jokers some time to cool off," Matthew counseled. "Take an extended trip."

"Yeah, it's nearly Passover," said James. "Why not make a quick trip to Jerusalem for Passover?"

The others all readily agreed.

Passover? Has a year really passed since I was last in Jerusalem for Passover? The days have flown by since I saw Nicodemus. They are like a blur, an endless stream of expectant faces, needy faces, faces marred by hatred.

"Well, Jesus," Peter said impatiently, "what'll it be?"

"I think Jerusalem is a splendid idea," I said. "Let's do it."

Accused of Blasphemy

This time, however, the going was much slower. I was surrounded by crowds everywhere I went. Some days I preached, others I spent exhausting hours healing those afflicted with horrible diseases and the countless demoniacs who were thrust in my presence. The demons were the worst, tormenting their hosts and physically abusing them.

We reached Jerusalem for the feast of the Jews a full week later—and on the Sabbath once again. I was so tired my legs felt like lead beneath me. Even my ever-present "honor guard" of Pharisees were hot and dusty. Still, I felt called to the Sheep Gate to a pool called Bethesda. Under the five tall covered Roman colonnades that surround it, some of Jerusalem's most desperately ill and disabled are brought—and left. There is a legend that when the waters of Bethesda are supernaturally stirred, the first one to enter the pool will be healed. And so the Holy City's blind, lame, deaf, paralyzed, and possessed are unceremoniously dumped here, day after day, blindly waiting for a miracle.

An old woman came up to us and said, "Master, do you see the invalid man in the corner? He has been left here virtually every day for the past thirty-eight years. Isn't there anything you can do?" Though she didn't say it, there is no mistaking a mother's love.

I walked over to the man, knelt down beside him and said, "My friend, do you want to be well?"

With great difficulty, he rolled his head to face me.

"Sir, I have no one to help me into the pool when the water is stirred. While I am trying to get in, someone else always goes down ahead of me."

His tone was one of resignation, not bitterness. He was merely stating a fact. He closed his eyes again and looked away.

Father, for his mother, and mothers who believe everywhere, please—heal this tortured soul.

Then I shouted, "Get up! Pick up your mat and walk!"

The man's head jerked up at the sound. He appeared to grow larger, like wine inflating a new skin. Within seconds, he stood on wobbly legs, shouting for everyone to see his newfound strength.

He grabbed up his filthy mat, danced a little jig, then sprang away from the pool—running headlong into a solid wall of shocked Pharisees who had seen the whole thing.

My old nemesis Bald Pharisee grabbed the man and snarled, "It is the Sabbath, you skinny fool! Don't you know that the law forbids you to carry your mat on the Sabbath?"

The once-paralyzed man shook with fear in the presence of so many Pharisees and said, "But...but the man who made me well said, 'Pick up your mat and walk.' "

Bald Pharisee smiled a cruel smile at his fellow Pharisees and said, "So, just who is this incredible healer who told you to pick it up and walk *on the Sabbath?*"

The frightened man turned and pointed a bony finger at where I had been standing just moments before.

But as soon as I saw Bald Pharisee, I slipped into the crowd and disappeared.

This is not the time nor the place for a confrontation with that *crew!* I thought uneasily.

Later that afternoon, I found the healed man on the Temple grounds, weaving slightly and stinking of cheap wine. He looked wildly about for any lurking Pharisees, then came gratefully over to me. He started to thank me, but I said, "You are indeed well again. But a word of advice: stop sinning or something worse could happen to you."

The man dropped his wine flask and started telling the Jews that I was the one who had healed him. When an excitable crowd began to gather, I figured I had better return to our inn for the evening.

Too late.

More Pharisees appeared—apparently materializing out of thin air! They formed a living wall around me and began shouting questions and accusations loud enough for everyone on the Temple grounds to hear.

"Ho, Nazarene!" one shouted, "what gives you the right to violate our sacred laws about work on the Sabbath?"

"My Father is always at his work to this very day," I responded. "And I, too, am working."

Several of the Pharisees cried out in anger and lunged at me, only to be restrained by Peter and Nathanael.

"Kill him!" they shouted. "Not only does he flagrantly break the Sabbath—he calls God his Father! He claims he is an equal with God! Blasphemy!"

"Stone him!" Fat Shanks howled. "Crucify him!"

Again they tried to attack me.

His hands full of vengeful Pharisees, Peter looked back over his shoulder and hissed, "Uhh, Jesus, *do* something here. This thing's kind of getting out of control!"

I had heard enough and seen enough.

"Listen!" I thundered—staring directly into the eyes of my accusers.

"Truly I tell you that the Son can do nothing by himself—nothing! He can do only what he sees his Father doing because whatever the Father does, the Son also does.

"For the Father loves his Son and shows him all he does. And, to your amazement, he will show him even greater things than these. For just as the Father raised the dead and gives them life, even so the Son gives life in whom he is pleased to give it."

I saw Nathanael beam happily. He was like a child in some ways, always looking for miracles and delighted when he found them. But Fat Shanks and Bald Pharisee were reddening.

"Besides all of that," I continued, "the Father judges no one, but has entrusted all judgment to the Son that all may honor the Son just as they honor the Father. He who does not honor the Son does not honor the Father—who sent him!

"Listen to me carefully: Whoever hears my word and believes him who sent me has eternal life and will not be condemned. That person has crossed over from death to life.

"People, a time is coming—and has now come—when the dead will hear the voice of the Son of God and those who hear will live. For as the Father has life in himself, so he has granted to the Son to have life in himself. And he has given him authority to judge because he is the Son of Man."

Even Peter grew saucer-eyed at this. Some of the Pharisees were muttering darkly among themselves and I saw more than one flash of metal—assassin's daggers! But I had no choice but to continue to speak.

"Do not be amazed at this, for a time is coming when all who are in their graves will hear his voice and come out—those who have done good will rise to live. But those who have done evil will rise to be condemned. Alone, I can do nothing: I judge only as I hear and my judgment is just—for I seek not to please myself but him who has sent me.

"You see, if I testify about myself, my testimony is not valid. There is another who testifies in my favor and I know that his testimony about me is valid."

I walked over to a small knot of Herodians, relatives and hangers-on of the cruel and fickle Roman puppet who ruled this land, even though he was not from Judea himself.

"You heard John the Baptist and he testified to the truth. Not that I accept human testimony, but I mention it that you may be saved. John is a lamp that burned bright and gave light and you chose for a time to enjoy his light.

"But I have testimony far weightier than that of John. For the very work that the Father has given me to finish, and which I am doing, *testifies* that the Father has sent me. And the Father who sent me has himself testified concerning me. You have never heard his voice nor seen his form, nor does his word dwell in you—for you do not believe the one he sent.

"Instead, you diligently study the Scriptures because you think that by them you possess eternal life. *And yet these are the very*

Scriptures that testify about me! And still you refuse to come to me to have life."

From the back, someone shouted, "You tell them, Jesus! How many lepers have *they* healed today?!"

Goat-beard tried to see who had shouted, so I walked up to him. He tried to glare at me, but was too nervous to pull it off.

"I do not accept praise from men, but I know you," I said. "I know that you do not have the love of God in your hearts. I have come in my Father's name and you do not accept me. But if someone else comes in his own name, you will accept him! How can you believe if you accept praise from one another, yet make no effort to obtain the praise that comes from the one and only God?"

A few of the Pharisees slipped out, doubtless to find some troublemakers to do their dirty work. It was time to wrap this up.

"But do not think I will accuse you before the Father," I said. "Your accuser is Moses! The same one on whom your hopes are all placed. If you believed Moses, then you should believe me— for he wrote about me!"

That did it! Goat-beard and Fat Shanks and the other Pharisees began screaming at me, calling for my death.

I motioned to my disciples to leave.

"But since you do not believe what he wrote," I said as I headed into the thickest part of the onlookers that surrounded us, "how are you going to believe what I say?"

JUDAS AND SIMON THE ZEALOT

We took the long way back around to the inn to avoid the mobs the Pharisees were stirring up. We glimpsed one of them by the market, shouting and hunting like a pack of dogs, questioning farmers about where they'd seen us last.

Eventually back at the inn, John said I had two visitors, Simon the Zealot and Judas Iscariot. Both said they wanted to join us.

Simon was an intense sort, a member of the Jewish underground, a transplanted Galilean fighting to end the Roman rule of Israel. Judas was handsome, articulate, charming, and witty. He said he was from Kerioth of Judea, but *iscariot* also means assassin's dagger and I knew of gangs of *sicarii* who used terrorist tactics in their opposition to Roman rule.

Both Simon and Judas had heard what I'd said to the Pharisees and were convinced that I was the man they wanted to follow.

Even as the others embraced Judas, something in the back of my mind kept nagging me about him.

Of course! His was one of the faces I had seen in the visions I had had in Bethabara and Cana! But in what capacity? And for what reason?

A sudden shout outside our inn shook me from my thoughts. One of the packs of troublemakers was dangerously close.

"At nightfall," I told Peter, "let's head back out into the countryside while things cool off here."

Then we would return to Galilee. We'd all had enough of the big city for a long, long time to come!

CHAPTER THREE

Spreading the Word

INSTRUCTING THE TWELVE

Back to Galilee we went. Once out of Jerusalem, large crowds began to tail behind us. Periodically, we would stop and I would teach and heal and—just as importantly—merely *listen* to what the people had to say. For many people, simply having someone take them seriously and listen to the stories of their lives was ministry enough.

After a while, we retreated to the hills outside Capernaum. I spent a tormented night in prayer, trying to discern my Father's will for those who would come after me. As dawn broke, I heard an answer. I rousted my twelve chosen followers and gathered them around me. As we huddled around the fire, I told them they would become my apostles. I said that they would carry on my message and take it to the far corners of the world, even beyond the Roman Empire, to lands yet unknown.

They all chattered excitedly about the future, laughing and joking. But as I looked in their faces—Peter, Andrew, Philip, Big James, John, Nathanael, Thomas, Thaddaeus, Simon the Zealot, Little James, Matthew, and Judas—I prayed desperately that their futures would be peaceful and prosperous.

"In the days ahead, I will ask you to go and preach this message," I told them gravely. "The kingdom of heaven is near." Go and heal the sick, raise the dead, cleanse those with leprosy, drive out demons.

"Freely you have been received, freely give. Do not take along any gold or silver or copper in your belts. Take no bag for the journey, or even an extra tunic or sandals or staff—for the worker is worth his keep.

"And whenever you enter a town, search for some worthy person there and stay at his house until you leave. When you enter that house, give it your greeting. If the home is deserving, let your peace rest on it. If it is not, let your peace return to you.

"But if anyone will not welcome you or listen to your words, shake the dust off your feet when you leave that home or town. My friends, I'm telling you that it will be more bearable in Sodom or Gomorrah on the day of judgment than for that town!"

All of the twelve's exuberance had vanished. All stared at me quizzically, none more so than Judas and Simon.

This isn't the path you expected your Messiah to take, is it, my friends? You dream of white chargers and marching armies and thousands cheering in Jerusalem! You dream of a conquering king to free Israel from Roman rule. There is much you've yet to learn.

"I am sending you out like sheep among wolves," I said. "Therefore, you're going to have to be as shrewd as snakes—and as harmless as doves.

"Even so, be on your guard against men. There are those who will hand you over to the local councils and flog you publicly in the synagogues.

"On my account you will be brought before governors and kings as witnesses to them and to the Gentiles. But when they arrest you—and they surely shall—do not worry about what to say or how to say it. You will be given the appropriate words at the time *and* how to say them. That's because it will not be you speaking, but the Spirit of the Father speaking through you."

All of their faces were ashen now, though only Simon and Judas showed any real disappointment.

But I wasn't through with them yet.

"You see, brother will betray brother to death, fathers will betray their children, and children will rebel against their parents—and have them put to death! All men will hate you because of me. But listen to me carefully now: he who stands firm to the end will be saved. When you are persecuted in one place, flee to another. Truly I tell you that you will not finish visiting all of the cities of Israel before the Son of Man comes."

I could see the questions forming on their faces.

"What I tell you in the dark, speak in the daylight. What is whispered in your ear, proclaim from the housetops. Do not be afraid of those who can kill your body—because they cannot kill your soul. Rather, only be afraid of those who can destroy your body *and* your soul.

"But remember this: Are not two sparrows sold for a penny? Yet not one of them will fall to the ground apart from the will of your Father. Even the very hairs of your head are numbered to him. So don't be afraid—you are worth much, much more than many sparrows!

"So whoever acknowledges me before men, I will also acknowledge him before my Father in heaven. But whoever disowns me before men, I will disown him before my Father in heaven."

I sat down and motioned them all closer. I could see the fear in their eyes. But what I had to tell them now was too important to hold any longer.

"Beloved friends, do not suppose for one instant that I have come to bring peace to the earth. I did *not* come to bring peace—but a sword! For I have come to turn, as it says in Micah,

Man against his father, a daughter against her mother, a daughter-
in-law against her mother-in-law—and a man's enemies will be
the members of his own household!

"Anyone who loves his father or mother more than me is not worthy of me. Anyone who loves his son or daughter more than me
is not worthy of me. Anyone who does not take his cross and follow me is not worthy of me. Whoever finds his life—will lose it.
Whoever loses his life for my sake—will find it."

ACCUSED OF BEING IN LEAGUE WITH THE DEVIL

The next morning, it was a shaken, somber, sober twelve that
accompanied me down the mountain. We quietly went into
Capernaum to Maariah's house. I hoped to spend a few quiet
moments with Peter's family before the crowds began to gather—
but to no avail. Within minutes, there were so many people
packed into the house that we were unable to eat.

Meanwhile, unbeknownst to me, someone—probably Bald
Pharisee, since he was originally from Nazareth—had sent word
to my family back in Nazareth, telling them all sorts of out-
landish stories about what I was doing and saying. And even as I
tried to teach in Maariah's house, my mother and brothers were
heading for Capernaum as quickly as possible.

So, with literally no other options—we couldn't have left the
house if we'd tried—I began teaching to those assembled. I had
barely begun when Goat-beard and a new Pharisee jumped up and
shouted, "Don't listen to this man—he is insane! Even his family thinks so! He is possessed by Beelzebub! He is driving out
demons with power given to him by the prince of demons!"

Out of the corner of my eye, I saw Andrew physically restrain
Peter from going after the new Pharisee (who Nathanael soon
dubbed—"Bushy-brows"). This was a new accusation, one that I

found unusually offensive. I'm afraid my exasperation with their attacks was beginning to show on my face and in my voice.

"How can Satan drive out Satan?" I sighed. "If a kingdom is divided against itself, that kingdom cannot stand. If a house is divided against itself, that house cannot stand. And if Satan somehow opposes himself and is then divided, then *he* cannot stand. His end has come.

"In fact, *no one* can enter a strong man's house and carry off his possessions—*unless he first ties up the strong man!* Then he can rob that house to his heart's content."

I fought to control my anger at these self-righteous, self-satisfied men.

"In truth," I said carefully, measuring my words, "all the sins and blasphemies of men will be forgiven them. But whoever blasphemes against the Holy Spirit will *never* be forgiven. This man is guilty of an *eternal* sin!"

This made even easygoing Judas shiver slightly!

"Now sit down and shut up!" Peter roared at the Pharisees. Whether it was my words or Peter's menacing demeanor—they did exactly that!

The rest of the day's preaching was less dramatic and, despite the brooding presence of the Pharisees, many believed.

But late that afternoon, there was a commotion outside Maariah's door. Someone shouted, "Let them pass! It's Jesus' family!"

Then someone near the door said, "Jesus! It's your mother and brothers. They've come looking for you. They say you're not well and want you to come back to Nazareth with them."

I could see Mary's face peering anxiously through the crush at the doorway. It saddened me that they had chosen to believe the lies about me—particularly after everything my mother had personally seen and heard since Bethlehem.

"Who are my mother and brothers?" I asked sadly. I motioned to those seated around me and standing against the walls. "*Here* are my mother and my brothers! Whoever does God's will is my brother and sister and mother."

And then Mary and my brothers left without me.

THE SERMON ON THE MOUNT

To spare poor Maariah more household chaos, we elected the following morning to go to the northeastern shore of the Sea of Galilee. After a short walk, we found a comfortable hillside with good acoustics. It had a small flat area where I could sit across a small ravine from another steep hillside where a multitude could hear and see easily. And so I began to teach and heal. As the day wore on, hundreds of people streamed to the hillside, some from as far away as Tyre and Jerusalem. Soon it was the largest crowd I'd ever spoken before.

"Blessed are you who are poor, for yours is the kingdom of God," I began. "Blessed are you who hunger now, for you will be satisfied. Blessed are you who weep now, for you will laugh. Blessed are you when men hate you, when they exclude you and insult you and reject your name as evil because of the Son of Man. *Rejoice* in that day and leap for joy because great is your reward in heaven. For *that* is how their fathers treated the prophets."

Still the people kept coming. My new disciples clustered around me, with Peter, Big James, and John—the unofficial leaders—sitting the closest.

"But woe to you who are rich, for you have already received your comfort," I continued. Several of the disciples good-naturedly—I think—poked Matthew. "Woe to you who are well-fed now, for you will go hungry. Woe to you who laugh now, for you will mourn and weep. Woe to you when all men speak well of you, for that is how their fathers treated the false prophets."

The great natural amphitheater had become so quiet that I could hear sheep bleating on a distant hill.

"But I'm telling you who hear me this day, *love* your enemies, *do good* to those who hate you, *bless* those who curse you, *pray* for those who mistreat you. If someone strikes you on one cheek, turn to him the other cheek. If someone takes your cloak, do not stop him from taking it. Give to everyone who asks you. And if anyone takes what belongs to you, do not demand it back. *In fact, do unto others as you would have them do unto you!*

"If you love those who love you—what credit is that to you? Even so-called sinners love those that love them. And if you do good only to those who are good to you—what credit is that to you? Even those same sinners do that. And if you lend to those from whom you expect repayment—what credit is that to you? Even sinners lend to other sinners, expecting to be repaid in full.

"But I'm telling you it is better to love your enemies, to do good to them, and lend to them without expecting to get anything back. *Then* your reward will be great, and you will be sons of the Most High because he is kind to the ungrateful and wicked. In short, be merciful—*just as your Father is merciful to you!*"

Again, I could tell by their faces that this wasn't sitting well with all those before me. Simon the Zealot and Judas in particular were squirming as they sat. These were men of action—not kind words!

"Do not judge, and you will not be judged," I said, louder than before. "Do not condemn, and then you will not be condemned. Forgive and you will be forgiven. Give and it will be given to you.

"A good measure, pressed down, shaken together and running over, will be poured into your lap. Because, people, it is with the measure that you use that *you* will be measured by.

"In other words, can a blind man lead a blind man? They will both fall into a hole, won't they? Likewise, a student can't be above his teacher. Only someone who is fully trained will be like his teacher.

"In short, why do you look at the speck of sawdust in your brother's eye—all the while paying no attention to the plank in your own eye?"

A ripple of laughter spread across the crowd.

"How can you say to your brother, 'Brother, here: Let me take the speck out of your eye' when you yourself fail to see the giant plank protruding from your own eye? You can't—you hypocrite! First you've got to take that plank out of your own eye; only *then* will you be be able to see clearly enough to remove the speck from your brother's eye."

This time it was Big James and John who nudged each other. Apparently, these brothers were more than a little competitive. It was time to change the tone.

"No good tree bears bad fruit," I continued, "nor does a bad tree bear good fruit. Instead, each tree is recognized by its own fruit—right? That means that people don't pick figs from thornbushes or grapes from briers. So, the good man brings good things out of the good stored up in his heart. The bad man, however, brings evil things out of the evil stored up in his heart. For out of the overflow of his heart does a man speak, whether it is good or bad.

"That's why I wonder about those of you that keep saying 'Lord, Lord'—and yet you do not do what I tell you.

"Let me tell you a story. This will show you what someone who comes to me and hears my words and *really* puts them into practice does. For that man is like someone who built a house. He dug deep into the ground and laid the foundation on solid rock. When the floods came and the torrent smashed against the house, it couldn't shake it—because it was so well built.

"Now, the man who hears my words and does *not* put them into practice is like yet another man who built yet another house nearby. But this man simply plopped his house on the ground, without building a foundation. When that same flood crashed against his house, it crumpled immediately and was swept away."

I spoke in this manner until nearly nightfall, quitting only to give the people time to return to their homes or find lodging in nearby Capernaum. I stayed a while longer healing those who asked for healing. Fortunately, practical Judas had thought to bring a torch, and after nightfall we were able to pick our way back into town, tired and famished. All I could think of was collapsing on my bed!

A DEAD MAN RAISED

We got a late start the next day for the nearby village of Nain. It didn't matter. Waiting outside Maariah's door were dozens of people and my familiar "bodyguard" of Pharisees, including Bushy-brows, who looked like he hadn't gotten much sleep that night, either! I found out later that his house was next to the centurion's—and the centurion and his family and friends celebrated the servant's new-found health until nearly dawn!

It was a pleasant early autumn day as my curious caravan traipsed through the Galilean countryside. But as we approached the old city gate of Nain, we saw a funeral procession coming. It appeared that half the town was in the procession. And judging by the number and fervor of the mourners, this was a well-loved person. We stepped off the road and assumed a posture of respect.

After a few moments, Little James whispered in my ear that this was the only son of a righteous widow. And then I saw her. My heart went out to her; she was devastated. She'd torn her clothes in anguish and her tears made black streaks through the ashes that covered her face and head.

Impulsively, I reached out a hand as she passed. "Don't cry," I said. I gripped her hand and gently led her back to the coffin. When the pallbearers saw me, they stopped in their tracks.

"Young man," I said loudly, "I say to you: Get up!"

Suddenly, there was a manic pounding from inside the casket! The startled pallbearers nearly dropped the casket in fright. But once it was on the road, several men worked feverishly to pry the lid off. In a heartbeat, a fist smashed through the wood from inside and tore the lid off.

The once-dead young man gratefully gulped noisy mouthfuls of air, then began looking wildly about for his mother. A great roar went up from those watching and many citizens surged forward to thank me. "A great prophet has appeared among us!" they shouted. "God has come to help his people!"

I looked about for Bushy-brows, but he had conveniently disappeared.

A QUESTION FROM JOHN

In Nain, the twelve and I were treated to a royal welcome and the entire town listened whenever I sat and talked. They were hungry for the Word and I was grateful for the opportunity to share it.

There were also a number of healings. With my Father's blessing, I was able to cast out some horrific demons as well.

That evening, two severe-looking men approached Simon. They spoke for long minutes, gesturing broadly and shooting glances my way.

At last, apparently satisfied that they were who they said they were, Simon cautiously led them to me. As they grew closer, I recognized them both. I'd seen them with John on the River Jordan. But both were now badly scarred and painfully thin.

I welcomed them warmly. I'd heard nothing of John since his imprisonment in Herod's cruel prison at Machaerus and was eager for news.

But the news was not good. John's disciples reported that he'd been savagely and systematically beaten, starved, and occasionally tortured.

I cried aloud.

"He has a message for you," the darker man said.

"Anything."

"He bids us ask, 'Are you the one who was to come, or should we expect someone else?' "

I felt a cold dagger pierce my soul.

Ahh, John. Once so strong, so sure, so steadfast. Has Herod broken your spirit as well as your body? May God have mercy on you, my beloved brother.

I smiled sadly at these brave followers.

"You have risked much to come here today," I said. "Please, go back with my blessing. Report to John what you have seen and heard: The blind receive sight, the lame walk, those who have leprosy are cured, the deaf hear, the dead are raised—*and the good news is preached to the poor.* Blessed is the man who does not fall away on account of me."

The thin, scarred men nodded and disappeared into the gathering darkness.

DINNER WITH BUSHY-BROWS

As I rose to leave, Bushy-brows walked up. I braced myself for another verbal assault. Judas moved to intercept the man, but I waved him off.

"Uh, Jesus, I realize we...uh...haven't been exactly on good terms or anything. But I've been...uh...thinking about what you just said about you and John the Baptizer. And I was wondering, that is, if you don't have other plans, if you'd perhaps join me for dinner tonight? But I'll understand if you can't—or won't," he added quickly.

I thought I heard Peter's jaw slam against his chest.

Behind Bushy-brows, Goat-beard and Bald Pharisee were staring daggers into his narrow back.

"I'd be delighted." And so the twelve of us ventured to Bushy-brows's house. Along the way we discovered that his name was Simon, son of Amzi.

Once inside, we all reclined around the well-stocked table and ate. Outside, as was often the case, townsfolk peered in through the windows and doors.

About midway through the meal, there was a slight disturbance at the door and before a servant could stop her, an exotically beautiful woman with lustrous black hair in braids that reached beyond her waist squeezed in through the press. She was carrying a simple alabaster jar that smelled of rich perfume.

Without a word, she knelt beside me at my feet and began weeping profusely in great, heaving sobs. The face of Simon, son of Amzi, contorted with anger and he motioned for his servants to throw her out—but I stopped them with a glance.

As her tears splashed on my dusty feet, she unbound her glorious hair and began tenderly wiping them. Then she bent over, kissed my feet, and began to pour on them a costly perfume from the jar.

I was speechless—but only partly because of what the woman was doing. I was "hearing" every thought that crossed Simon the Pharisee's mind: *Well, if this Jesus really knew who this little tramp was and what she did for a living, you better believe he wouldn't let her massage his feet! What kind of prophet allows harlots—unrepentant sinners—to make a spectacle of a so-called holy man?*

I resisted my first impulse to lash out at him. Instead, I called Simon over.

"Simon, son of Amzi," I said in a voice loud enough even for those outside to hear, "I have something to tell you."

Simon, never taking his eyes off the gorgeous woman, said through gritted teeth, "Tell me, Teacher."

"Two men owed money to a certain moneylender. One owed him five hundred denarii and the other owed him fifty denarii. Neither, alas, could pay him back. So the moneylender, in a fit of charity, cancelled both their debts. Simon, which of the debtors will love the charitable moneylender more?"

"Why, I suppose the man who had the bigger debt cancelled—right?"

"Exactly right," I said. Then I turned and faced the weeping woman directly, but kept speaking to Simon:

"Simon, do you see this woman?"

He snorted his disgust by way of assent.

"I came into your house as your guest, Simon the Pharisee, son of Amzi. *You* did not give me any water for my feet. But she has wet my feet with her tears and wiped them with her hair. *You* did not give me a kiss, but this woman, from the time I entered, has not stopped kissing my feet. *You* did not put oil on my head, but she has poured perfume on my feet!

"Therefore, I'm telling you that her many sins have been forgiven—for she has loved much. *But he who has been forgiven little loves little.*"

I tilted her tear-stained chin up so that she was looking me straight in the eye.

"Go," I said, "your sins are forgiven."

Simon, all pretense of civility now lost, whirled to another guest and sneered, "Who is this who even forgives sins?"

But I never took my eyes off the lovely weeping woman. "Your faith has saved you. Go in peace, little one."

Shortly thereafter, we thanked the still-sputtering Simon, son of Amzi, for his hospitality, and retired to a nearby inn. I thought we had a fleeting window of opportunity with poor Simon, but his self-righteousness, alas, won out in the end.

THE KINGDOM OF HEAVEN

When I left the next morning with the twelve to continue my mission in Galilee, a large crowd was already waiting. Among them, perhaps because of what had happened to the weeping woman, were a significant number of women. Women who dared follow me were extraordinarily brave. Besides the usual hardships, they risked banishment from their families and a thousand and one lies spread about them. But from that moment forward, women comprised the majority of the crowds that followed me. And I was delighted.

Several women in particular became fast friends. First there was Mary, who had traveled from Magdala to be exorcised of seven hideous demons. Then there was Joanna, wife of Chuza, the manager of Herod's sprawling household. Joining the strong-willed Susanna were several other equally brave, steadfast women. Mary, Joanna, and Susanna financially supported a number of women so that they could travel and learn from me. And Joanna's access to news from Herod's court was unparalleled—and extremely valuable.

All were with us as we traveled from Nain northeast, stopping in every little settlement, preaching and healing as we went.

At the end of the first day, a huge crowd spread before me and I was forced to climb to the roof of a modest home nearby to be seen and heard. Near the end of the day, Mary Magdalene asked, "Teacher, just what *is* the kingdom of heaven?"

"It is easier to describe in parable form," I answered. "See if this helps:

"The kingdom of heaven is like a treasure hidden in a field. When a certain man found that treasure, he hid it again and then immediately sold all he had to buy that field.

"Here's another way of thinking of it:

"The kingdom of heaven is like a merchant looking for fine pearls. When he found one of great value, he went away and auctioned everything he had—and bought it."

Mary Magdalene happily nodded her understanding, but several of my disciples kept staring at me blankly.

"Then think of it this way," I said. "The kingdom of heaven is like a net that was let down into the lake and caught all kinds of fish. When it was full, the fisherman pulled it up on the shore. Then they sat down and collected the good, edible fish in baskets and threw the others back.

"That, you see, is how it will be at the end of the age. The angels will come and separate the wicked from the righteous and throw the wicked into the fiery furnace where there will be weeping and wailing and gnashing of teeth."

Still no glimmer of recognition among some of the disciples. So I tried again:

"The kingdom of heaven is like a farmer who sowed good seed in his field. But that night, while he slept, his enemies crept onto his lands and sowed weeds among the wheat. That spring, when the wheat sprouted, so did the weeds.

"When it was clear what was happening, his servants rushed to him and said, 'Sir, didn't you plant good seed in your fields? Where did these weeds come from?'

"The farmer replied, 'I fear it must have been sown by one of our enemies.'

"The servants asked, 'Do you want us to go and pull them up?'

"But the farmer said, 'No, because while you are pulling up the weeds, you may uproot the wheat with them. Instead, let both grow together until the harvest. At that time I will instruct the harvesters to first collect the weeds and tie them in bundles to be burned, *then* to gather the wheat and bring it into my barn.'

"And that is what the kingdom of heaven is like."

But it was clear from the frowns of concentration in the audience that my parables still weren't sinking in.

"Okay," I said, "let me explain it yet another way. The kingdom of heaven is like the yeast that a woman took and mixed into a large amount of flour until it worked all through the dough."

Still no sign of recognition from most of my listeners, save for a few of the educated women and perhaps John, Big James, and Peter. But even they didn't look too sure!

Unfortunately, sunset was fast approaching. I would have to leave this teaching for another day.

"Let me try one last time," I said. "A farmer went out to sow his seed. As he was scattering the seed, some fell along the path and the birds came and snatched it up immediately.

"Some of the seed fell on rocky places where there was only a thin layer of soil. Those plants sprang up quickly, but were scorched in the sun and withered because they had such shallow roots.

"Still more seed fell among thorns, which grew up and choked the young plants.

"But the rest of the seed fell on fertile ground and it produced a crop of a hundred, or sixty, or thirty times what was sown.

"Those with ears, let them hear."

TEACHING IN PARABLES

After the bulk of the crowd drifted away, my disciples and a few of the others sat with me around our fire. After some hemming and hawing around, Nathanael finally said what was on everybody's mind:

"Uh, Master, why *do* you speak to the people in parables? I mean, wouldn't a simple answer carry...uh...carry more weight?"

I said, "The knowledge of the kingdom of heaven has been given to you all, but not yet to them. You see, whoever has been given more, he will have an abundance. Whoever does not have, even what he has will be taken away from him.

"So, this is why I speak to them in parables: 'Though seeing, they do not see; though hearing, they do not understand.'

"It's like what the prophet Isaiah once said: 'You will be ever hearing, but never understanding; you will be ever seeing but never perceiving. For this people's heart has become calloused; they bare-ly hear with their ears, and they have closed their eyes. Otherwise they might see with their eyes, hear with their ears, understand with their hearts and turn—and I would heal them.' "

Nathanael started to speak, but I motioned to him to listen a moment longer.

"But blessed are your eyes because they see; and your ears because they hear. For I tell you the truth, many prophets and righteous men longed to see what you see but did not see it; and to hear what you hear but did not hear it."

"That's all well and good, Rabbi," Nathanael said quickly. "But I still don't get what the parable of the sower *means*. I just don't get it. Does that make me stupid?"

A few others laughed at Nathanael's statement, but it was the uneasy laughter of people who didn't really understand either.

"No, you are certainly not stupid, Nathanael," I said gently. "This is what that parable means: When anyone hears the message about the kingdom and does not understand it, the Evil One comes and snatches away what was sown in his heart. This is the seed sown along the path.

"What was sown on the rocky places is the man who hears the Word and at once receives it with joy. But since he has no root, he lasts only a short time. When trouble or persecution comes because of the Word, he quickly falls away.

"What was sown among the thorns is the man who hears the Word, but the worries of this life and the deceitfulness of wealth choke it, making it unfruitful.

"But what was sown on good soil is the man who hears the Word and understands it. He produces a crop yielding a hundred, sixty or thirty times what was sown."

"All right, Teacher, that makes sense," Thaddaeus said, "but I still can't make hide nor hair of the parable of the weeds—you know, the one where the farmer's enemies try to destroy his crop with weeds. I *think* I got it, but maybe some of the others might not have...uh...figured it out so quickly."

I had to smile at Thaddaeus's obvious discomfort.

"That's all right," I said. "You're probably right.

"The one who sowed the good seed is the Son of Man. The field is the world and the good seed represents the sons of the kingdom. The weeds are the sons of the Evil One and the enemy who sows them is the devil. The harvest is the end of the age and the harvesters are the angels."

I tossed another large branch into the fire, causing flickering sparks to float toward the heavens.

"As the weeds are pulled up and burned in the fire, so it will be at the end of the age. The Son of Man will send out his angels and they will weed out of his kingdom everything that causes sin and all who do evil. They will throw them into the fiery furnace. Then the righteous will shine like the sun in the kingdom of the Father. Again, he who has ears, let him hear.

"Have you understood all of these things?" I asked them all after this had had time to sink in.

"Yes," most of them said, although not with a lot of enthusiasm.

"Good," I said, "then every teacher of the law who has been instructed about the kingdom of heaven is like the owner of a house who brings out of his storeroom new treasures as well as old."

"Aww, he did it to us again," Nathanael griped to Andrew, who stifled a snicker.

CALMING A STORM

Still, the days that followed were successful ones. We traveled freely about Galilee, speaking to large groups of people and healing many. Even as the weather turned colder, the faithful turned out to listen and learn. Even the Pharisees remained steadfast—although we never saw Bushy-brows again.

I felt it was time to cross to the other side of the Sea of Galilee to visit the towns of the Decapolis, so the fishermen of the twelve volunteered their boats to ferry us all across. But as we were preparing to embark, a Pharisee approached me. We'd seen him before, but he'd never joined in the sport of baiting or taunting me in public.

"Teacher," he said, "I will follow you wherever you go."

"My friend," I said, "foxes have their holes and the birds of the air have their nests, but the Son of Man has no place to lay his head."

That gave him pause. He stood there, pondering the implications of what I said.

Moments later, one of the men who had been following us for several weeks came up.

I said, "Kohath! Good of you to come. Why don't you accompany us across the lake? There is a rich harvest awaiting us on the eastern shore."

He said, "Lord, first let me go and bury my father."

I placed my hand on his shoulder. "Kohath, follow me now. And let the dead bury their own dead."

But as I feared he would, Kohath sadly shook his head and departed, never to return.

At last we set off. Ominous clouds were approaching from the Great Sea to the west, but Peter and John were confident we could easily beat any storm. Still exhausted from the previous few days, I retired below decks to grab a few hours of long-overdue sleep.

But John and Peter were wrong.

Sharp, cold winds suddenly blasted us from the west as black, oily clouds bubbled and foamed overhead. Within minutes we were locked in a full-blown gale, with waves hammering our decks. I must have been more tired than I thought, because they tell me I slept peacefully through the roughest seas.

At last, as water began pouring in through the hold, Little James and Philip despaired of ever seeing land again and woke me.

"Lord! Lord! Save us!" Philip cried. "We're going down! We're all going to die!"

Sleepily, I accompanied them to the deck, where Peter had tethered himself. He too began screaming for me to save them.

"Oh you of little faith," I said, shouting above the wind, "why are you so afraid?"

Then I turned and faced the angry sea and rebuked the wind and waves.

The pressure dropped so quickly, my ears popped. The waves rose, then faltered, then spread out like oil on water. The winds surged upward, scattering the clouds above us. In seconds, the late autumn sun blasted through, warming our cold and soaked bodies.

John grabbed his brother and whispered frantically, "What kind of man is this? Even the winds and waves obey him!"

A LEGION OF PIGS

The storm had blown us slightly off course, so that we landed in the country of the Gadarenes, near the tombs of their dead. In the higher ground above the tombs, we could see herdsmen tending a herd of swine. But before we'd even secured the boats, two men came howling out of the tombs toward us.

They were a frightening sight: dressed in bloody rags, covered in sores, their ragged hair streaming behind them, and gibbering like banshees.

"Unclean!" Nathanael hollered. "Undead *and* unclean!"

The two snarling, drooling men stood defiantly before us, blocking our way to the road. The hapless men were clearly possessed by many malignant devils. Simon the Zealot leaped to my side, pulling his cruel assassin's dagger. Peter too stepped forward, gripping his sword.

One of the demoniacs still had the remains of chains and shackles attached to his wrists and ankles.

"What do you want with us, Son of God?" he roared in the voice of a thousand demons, the foul stench of his breath staggering us all. "Have you come here to torture us before the appointed time?"

But before I could cast the demons out, one of the men fell groveling at my feet. "Swear that you won't torture us, Son of the

Most High God! If you drive us out, at least send us into that herd of pigs!"

I had no intention of allowing several thousand demons loose in the land. Still, I said, "What is your name?"

And amid the babble of responses, one voice boomed through, "My name is Legion, for we are many!"

"Come out of these men, you evil spirits!" I shouted.

The two men fell like broken puppets, then there was a faint smell of brimstone and rotten eggs and a slight, ever-so-slight, breeze. Immediately, the pigs on the hill began tearing and slashing at each other. The herdsmen jumped atop boulders to escape the bloody carnage. Then, as if with one mind, the poor animals stampeded toward a cliff overlooking the rocky beach below!

The dumbfounded herdsmen dashed back toward the nearby village of the Gadarenes, as did the two poor souls who had been possessed.

After we'd safely secured our boats and repaired the worst of the storm damage, we headed toward the Gadarene village. We had barely passed the tombs when we were met by a noisy mob of people, led by the herdsmen.

"Leave us in peace, Jesus of Nazareth!" some shouted in fear. Others begged that we leave. Still others threatened us if we came further.

"We will go nowhere we are not wanted," I told the town's leaders, and we walked back to the sea amid a halfhearted rain of rotten vegetables and small stones.

Back at the boats, the man with chains came whimpering up. "Please, let me go with you, Master," he said.

But I answered, "No, go home to your family and tell them how much the Lord has done for you—and how he has mercy on you."

When the man had reluctantly left, I told the sailors, "Set sail for Capernaum. We're going home."

JAIRUS'S DAUGHTER

This time the sea cooperated and we made good time. As we sailed up, someone recognized our boats and spread the word in town, so by the time we disembarked, a small crowd was already there to greet us.

As I walked away from the docks, a wealthy man came running up and knelt before me. "Master," he said, staring at the ground, "my name is Jairus and my daughter is dying. Please come and put your hand on her—and she will live!"

I took Jairus's hand and lifted him to his feet. "Lead the way," I said, and we followed him toward his house.

But with every step of the way, more and more people gathered around us. Soon it became a small army, slowing our progress to a crawl. And amidst all of the jostling and solid press of people, a single frail woman snaked a hand through the crowd and touched the hem of my garment.

The healing power flowed out of me in a warm stream. I stopped the unruly procession. "Who touched my clothes?" I demanded.

Simon the Zealot said, "Teacher, there must be hundreds of people crowding around us, all reaching for you. How can you ask, 'Who touched me?'"

But I kept scanning the faces of those closest to me.

After a heartbeat, the woman who had touched me managed to push her way through and fell at my feet.

"Master! I touched you. Forgive me. I've been bleeding uncontrollably for the past twelve years. I've suffered from the 'treatments' of a variety of doctors and only gotten worse. When I heard you were back in town, I thought, 'If I can just but touch his clothes, I will be healed!' And that's what happened! I've been healed, praise God!"

I sat down beside her. "Daughter, your faith has healed you. Go in peace and be freed from your suffering."

Before we could resume our passage toward Jairus's house, several important men from the synagogue shouted that they needed to see me immediately. They roughly pushed their way through the surging crowd and found me still sitting next to the woman and near the increasingly impatient Jairus.

"Jairus, our brother, sad news," one said. "My friend, your beloved daughter is dead."

Jairus sank in a heap beside us, great sobs of grief wracking his body.

The others put their arms around him to lead him home. "No need to bother the Teacher anymore. Let us go and begin the burial rites."

I stepped between the synagogue leaders and Jairus. "Wait," I said. "Don't be afraid, Jairus. Just believe."

We walked as quickly as we could to Jairus's house. Once there, I bid the crowd to wait, then walked through the door with Peter, James, John, and the grief-stricken Jairus. Inside the house, the screams of pain and grief were nearly deafening. Professional mourners vied with the family to see who could wail the loudest. Flute players played mournful dirges in minor keys.

I shouldered my way to the young girl's bedside, where she lay as pale as a spring lily.

"Why all this commotion and wailing?" I demanded. "The child is not dead, but asleep!"

The professional mourners laughed bitterly and insulted me, flinging themselves dramatically on the girl's bed to the accompaniment of the minor-key pipes.

"Jairus, clear the room," I said. Uncomprehending, Jairus still obeyed. Now only Jairus, his wife, and the four of us stood by the cold body.

I took her hand and said softly to her, "Little girl, I say to you, 'Get up!' "

At that moment, her eyes fluttered open and she stretched a most delicious stretch. Then she bounded out of bed—I'd say she was about twelve—smiled at all of us and said politely to her mother, "Mother, is there anything to eat? I'm starved!"

Even the serious-minded John leaped for joy and danced madly with the girl's parents.

I took them aside and warned them not to tell anyone what they had seen.

"Now, feed that poor child," I said with a smile. "She hasn't eaten in days!"

MORE HOSTILITY IN NAZARETH

We decided it was time to visit the small villages along the Kishon River, just west of Nazareth and southeast of Mt. Carmel. I had only been there once before and the people had seemed eager to hear the word.

So leaving the familiar confines of Capernaum, we set out once again, a portion of the huge crowd still patiently dogging my every footstep.

Perhaps the reason we'd only gone to the Kishon Valley once before was that the only way there was through Nazareth.

But the press of people was so great and their needs so many, that it was the Sabbath once again when we reached the edge of town.

Nathanael in particular argued for us to simply pass through Nazareth as quickly and quietly as possible. He remembered all too well how close to death we'd been here in my former hometown.

But Bald Pharisee and Goat-beard had other plans. A delegation of Pharisees met us outside the city and invited us—once again—to teach at the synagogue. I huddled briefly with the twelve.

"It's a trap," Nathanael wailed.

"We'll be ready this time," Simon the Zealot said coldly, fingering his wickedly curved dagger.

I frowned at Simon.

"No weapons in the synagogue," I warned Simon.

"Still, I'll give no man the opportunity to say that I fear the synagogue of my people, or that I am too frightened to spread the message God has given me."

And so we filed uneasily into the synagogue of Nazareth. The Pharisees, with great ceremony and mock courtesy, extended me the scrolls, and I began to teach.

Within moments, there was a loud murmuring among those in attendance.

"What's this wisdom that's been given him that does miracles?" one said loudly.

"Hey! Isn't this Jesus the carpenter?" asked another.

"Yeah—it's Mary's son, the brother of James, Joseph, Judas, and Simon! And look—his sisters are here with us!"

"Who cares what ol' Jesus has to say?"

"I hear he's a blasphemer."

"Stone him!"

I gingerly placed the scrolls back in their appointed places and bowed to the threatening congregation.

"Only in his hometown, among his relatives, and in his own house, is a prophet without honor," I said, and then left.

I healed a few more demoniacs and lepers on the way out of town, but most people gave us a wide berth. After all we'd seen—and done—in Galilee, the lack of faith and outright hostility in Nazareth still amazed me.

Fortunately, our stay in the villages of the Kishon Valley was more productive. We spoke long and often to appreciative listeners and were able to heal many who came for help.

My disciples—all twelve of them—had been growing in the Word each day and had become a great aid to me. The many villages along the Kishon were the perfect opportunity for them. There were few Pharisees about and the people were friendly and receptive.

So I called them all together, told them to pair up, and sent them to visit as many villages as possible, preaching repentance.

Over the next few weeks, that's exactly what they did, going from town to town, driving out demons, anointing the sick with oil and healing them, and preaching the good news of our Father's love for a repentant people. I was thrilled with their maturity—and success. We planned to spend the winter there.

JOHN THE BAPTIST BEHEADED

But after the incident in Nazareth's synagogue, Goat-beard and Bald Pharisee had apparently seen enough. According to Joanna, who had sources throughout Herod's palace, Bald Pharisee had scurried to Herod's palace at Machaerus and told of my growing power and popularity in dangerous terms.

"See what that awful John started," his wife Herodias (formerly the wife of Philip, his brother) had purred to Herod. "It's all John's fault with the lies he's been telling about us. Why don't you just have him killed and be done with it?"

But Joanna's steward said that Herod still secretly went to the dungeon and consulted with John, for even in chains and broken, Herod respected John's fierce honesty.

Time and again, Herod rebuffed Herodias's attempts to have John murdered. But Joanna said that Herodias had had another plan in the works for some time.

In the days that followed, Herod hosted a mammoth party for the Roman high officials and military commanders of Galilee. For a man with as tenuous a hold on the throne as Herod, these parties were of supreme importance.

Herodias arranged the entertainment, including a dance by Salome, her beautiful daughter—who Joanna said Herod had openly lusted after. Herodias had spent weeks preparing for the dance—the lighting, the incense, the sensuous music, even the revealing, gossamer costume. Then she had Salome rehearse strenuously.

The night of the party, Salome's dance was the featured entertainment. Joanna said that Salome danced with sexual abandon, flirting and teasing Herod without shame. The Romans roared their approval and showered her with expensive gifts.

At last, Salome glided up to Herod and assumed a most provocative pose as the music died.

Herod jumped to his feet and—noting the gifts of his sex-crazed guests—grandly pronounced, "Ask me for anything you want, dear girl, and I'll give it to you! This I swear in front of our esteemed guests and great Zeus himself!"

The drunken Romans applauded the grand gesture.

Salome bowed deeply, then went to her mother, who was standing nearby.

"What shall I ask for?" she said breathlessly.

Herodias smiled. She had won.

"Ask for the head of John the Baptist," she said.

As Salome returned to the throne, Herodias quietly signaled for the musicians to begin the hot-blooded themes once again.

Salome sat teasingly on Herod's lap and announced in a loud voice, "I want the head of John the Baptist on a platter—now!"

The Romans brayed and howled like animals, toasting Salome and hooting at Herod.

"That is," Salome whispered in his ear, "if you're man enough."

Joanna said Herod stammered a few minutes, then reluctantly sent his executioners to the dank prison. A few minutes later, the chief executioner returned, carrying the dark and scarred head of John the Baptist on a silver tray.

Herodias squealed her delight and danced with the head around the room. But by now, most of the Romans were asleep in drunken stupors, leaving Herod alone to brood on his deeds that night.

When Joanna finished her horrific tale, I excused myself and prayed—and cried—for the rest of the day, hidden in a copse of bare trees overlooking the Kishon, oblivious to the cold winds howling from the north.

With the murder of John, another milestone in my life had passed.

I was another step closer to understanding those strange, grotesque images I had seen in my visions.

And when I emerged, the wind had changed.

Perhaps forever.

CHAPTER FOUR

Transformations

LOAVES AND FISHES

As winter turned to spring, the apostles began returning to the appointed place. They me told of the wonders they'd seen—and done—of families and entire villages saved, of demons sent squalling back into the void, of the Word preached throughout the land.

And along with the twelve came hundreds of others, following in vast numbers, all eager to listen and learn. As before in Capernaum, the crush of people eventually grew so great that we were unable to move freely.

It was time to return to Capernaum in Galilee.

But the absence had not dimmed the ardor of those who loved the Word and as soon as we were back in town, thousands more flocked around us.

The twelve were mentally and physically tired, so I asked the fishermen in the group to loan us one of their boats once again and we tried to slip out into the Sea of Galilee, looking for a quiet place to land—and rest. We heard of just such a barren place near Bethsaida and that's where we put ashore.

But again we were recognized and word spread like wildfire to the villages and towns to the north of the Sea of Galilee. Those who heard raced to find us. Entire villages trooped across the barren and inhospitable land and, once they found us, began milling around aimlessly, waiting for me to speak.

So I found a small rock outcropping and began teaching, praying for strength and wisdom with every spare breath.

My Father must have answered my prayers because before I knew it, the afternoon shadows were lengthening. I had spent the entire day in teaching and ministering and many had been touched by the Word.

During a pause, Matthew came up and said, "Master, this is a remote, barren place and it's already very late. Maybe we better send the people away so they'll have time to get to the surrounding villages and buy something to eat."

Oh, practical Matthew, I thought, *it is good to have you along. Every group needs an accountant like you.*

But I said, "No, *you* give them something to eat."

His eyebrows shot up. "Uh, Master, that would take eight months of a man's wages! Are we to go and spend that much on bread and give it to them to eat?"

I could see the wheels turning in his head, calculating how much money they could raise, how far it would go, how they would transport the bread from Bethsaida back here, where the funds would come from for the rest of the journey.

"No," I said, "there is something better we can do. Take the other disciples and count the number of loaves there are among the multitude assembled here."

Still shaking his head, Matthew did just that. A few minutes later he came back, crestfallen over the prospect of feeding this crowd.

"Only five loaves, Lord," he said, "and two fish. Shall I leave for Bethsaida?"

"No, I want you and the other disciples to arrange the people comfortably in the fields in groups of fifty and a hundred. Leave plenty of room between the groups so that we may pass easily between them. Then return to me with those five loaves and two fish."

By now, Matthew was utterly perplexed. But, as always, he did exactly as he was told. When he was through, the multitude was arranged in perfect rows and squares—no Roman centurion could have done better! He'd also gathered hundreds of empty baskets of varying shapes and sizes.

I sat with the disciples and began praying, thanking my Father for the food, and blessing the bread and fish as I broke them and passed the pieces to the disciples on either side of me. Then someone from each group came to the end of the line and picked up several baskets of food.

"I do this in your name, Father," I said.

Matthew coordinated the process, barking orders, calling for empty baskets, making sure everyone was fed.

And, when we were finished, everyone *was* fed through God's grace.

Matthew reported back to me that there were even twelve baskets of bread and fish left over.

"How many did the five loaves and two fish feed, Matthew?" I asked him.

He did some quick calculations in his head. "I must confess I was too busy carrying food to count everyone, Lord," he said. "But I do know that we fed at least five thousand men."

"Great," I said. "*Now* you may send them home."

But the people who had been fed had other ideas. They began to talk among themselves. Soon they whipped themselves into a frenzy.

"Surely, this is the prophet who is to come into the world!" one shouted.

"This man has powers far beyond ours!" said another.

"This Jesus needs to lead us!" said still another.

But when they began chanting, "Hail King Jesus! Hail King Jesus!" I knew it was time to act. I had no intention of being made a king by force!

So, under the cover of the settling darkness, I withdrew to the mountainside behind me. Without my presence, the crowd gradually dispersed.

Flickering torches spreading out in all directions showed me that most of the enormous crowd was heading for home, so I returned down from the mountain. I met the twelve and others who remained by the boat.

"The feeding of the five thousand has come at great cost," I told them. "I need some time alone to pray and regain my strength. The rest of you pull out offshore a ways where the waves are still and sleep. I'll be fine. We'll meet again in Capernaum in a couple of days."

Over Judas's protests, they put out to sea. After I'd waved goodbye, I took a torch and went up into the hills alone.

WALKING ON WATER

But later that evening, the wind picked up and blew the boat further out into the dark Sea of Galilee, waking the men and forcing them to the oars.

The sound of the wind roused me from my prayers and I walked back to the shore. I could see their faint lanterns near the middle of the lake. They were straining to make toward the shelter of the port in Capernaum, but it was a losing battle.

Ahh, my poor friends. Instead of a night of rest, you get a night of work and stress.

So I walked across the water to them, my own torch whipping in the fresh spring winds.

As I approached the boat, I heard screams of fear, like souls in torment! They had seen me and feared that I was a ghost approaching them.

"Flee! Flee!" I heard Judas cry. "It's a ghoul from the tombs coming to eat us!"

"Wait!" I shouted, a little hurt by their lack of faith.

What did the feeding of the five thousand mean to them? Did they learn nothing about me? Have they learned nothing in the past year?

"Take courage! It is I, Jesus! Don't be afraid."

By the boat's pale lamps, I could just make out the burly form of Peter leaning over the railing, staring at me.

"Lord, if that's *really* you, tell me to come to you across the water," he said.

"Come, Peter," I shouted back.

To my delight, he climbed over the side of the boat and, after tentatively placing his foot on the water, began walking rapidly toward me.

Just then, a stray gust of wind whipped up the waves. For whatever reason, it must have caused him to lose faith. He sank like a stone.

"Lord, save me!" he yelled.

I ran over to him and, with my free hand, pulled him from the waves. Together, the two of us walked to the boat where the others helped us aboard.

It was an awkward moment, standing there in the weirdly flickering light, out in the middle of the Sea of Galilee. I didn't know if the disciples were ashamed, or frightened, or simply stunned. Matthew had the presence of mind to wrap a warm coat around Peter, who sat shivering on the deck.

Then John kneeled down before me and said, "Truly, you *are* the Son of God." The others promptly followed suit.

But Judas continued to eye me suspiciously. I knew what he was thinking: "If this man can so nonchalantly walk on water and feed five thousand, why can't he save his own people from slavery?" But he never broached the subject with me and I respected his privacy.

THE BREAD OF LIFE

My arrival with the twelve in Capernaum caused something of a sensation. Too many had seen me *not* get on the boat—and yet here I was. I'd barely left the docks when a large crowd formed.

"Rabbi, when did you get here?" one woman asked.

I said, "You've been looking for me, not because you saw miraculous signs, but because you ate the loaves and had your fill. Do not work for food that spoils, but instead for the food that endures. This is the food of eternal life. This is the food that the Son of Man will give you. God the Father has placed his seal of approval on him."

The woman digested this a moment, then said, apparently speaking for a number of people in the crowd: "What must we do to do these works that God requires?"

"The work of God is just this," I answered. "Believe in the one he has sent."

"That's all well and good," someone shouted from the back of the ever-growing crowd. "But what miraculous sign then will you give us that we may see it and believe you? What will *you* do? After all, our forefathers ate the manna in the desert. As it was written, 'He gave them bread from heaven to eat.' "

The crowd was getting unruly; a shoving match erupted at the fringes. I could see several familiar Pharisee faces forcing their way to the front. This was not an ideal setting for a serious teaching, but I could tell that there were some in the crowd who were honestly searching—and so very, very close to understanding.

"I tell you the truth," I said carefully, "it is not Moses who has given you the bread from heaven, but my Father in heaven who gives you the *true* bread from heaven. For the bread of God is he who comes down from heaven and gives life to the world."

The first woman, now nearly swallowed by the jostling crowd, reached a hand toward me and said, "Sir, from now on, give us this bread!"

In a moment she would be gone. I had no choice. I had to speak plainly *now*—whatever the cost.

"Listen!" I said. "*I* am the bread of life. He who comes to me will never go hungry. He who believes in me will never be thirsty. But, as I've already told you, you have seen me and still many of you do not believe. All that the Father gives me will come to me, and whoever comes to me I will never drive away. For I have come down from heaven not to do my will, but to do the will of him who sent me.

"And *this* is the will of him who sent me, that I shall lose none of all that he has given me, but raise them up at the last day. For my Father's will is that everyone who looks to the Son and believes in him shall have eternal life—and I will raise him up on the last day!"

Then she was gone, lost in the crush of people, elbowed aside by larger, rougher hands. I never saw her again. But in our last, fleeting eye contact, I saw that she *knew*. And I was relieved.

But in the meantime, the crowd had turned into a mob, a mob incited by Bald Pharisee and Goat-beard.

SOMETHING IN THE WIND

We all agreed it was past time to leave Capernaum, so we took the boat again and crossed the Sea of Galilee to Gennesaret. Even as we were dropping anchor, people began to gather along the wharf. By the time we were ashore, the harbor was full of desperate, needy people. It became like some fantastic open-air hospital. Every open place in the city was filled with the pallets of the lame, the blind, the dying. Lepers hobbled toward us from all directions on gangrene-ridden stumps. Demons cursed and snarled as we passed, their hosts slumped in doorways and street corners.

My disciples and I fanned through the city, seeing, touching, healing as many as humanly possible. At nightfall, we slept where we were, surrounded by the moans and cries of the afflicted.

As I staggered through the marketplace later that week, Judas ran up to me and grabbed my tunic.

"By the Father! Jesus, we must leave here! I can't stand it any longer. We are all being sucked dry. These people are like leeches. We can't heal them all!"

"No, we can't," I said wearily, stopping to touch the head of a child suffering from seizures, "but we can heal this one."

And her seizures stopped.

In time, we did manage to work our way through the city and into the countryside. Once there, we were able to do more preaching and less healing, though people still thronged wherever we went, groping just to touch the hem of my cloak.

We slowly moved northeast, up around the eastern and northern shores of the Sea of Galilee, working our way back to Capernaum once again. Simon and Judas counseled vigorously against it.

"You're not safe there, Lord," Simon said. "We can't guarantee your safety. Those idiot Pharisees have the people too worked up against you!"

"But where else can I go, Simon?" I asked. "Nazareth? Bethlehem? Jerusalem? No, for now I must return because it is as close to a home as I have. There is no place else."

And while the crowds were still growing as we walked, I felt a gathering unease in my spirit. So much had changed so quickly. Perhaps it was John's murder that continued to cast a pall on all of us. Perhaps it was the loss of so many followers in Capernaum. Perhaps it was the brooding, ever-scowling face of Judas. Or perhaps there really was something in the wind.

WHAT IS CLEAN?

Perhaps this *was* a good time to visit Phoenicia. So we left Galilee and walked northwest to Tyre, one of the two largest Phoenician cities. This time, even the disciples noticed that the crowds were thinning.

THE SYRO-PHEONICIAN WOMAN

My goal was to rest for a time at a friend's house in Tyre and get my strength back. We came into this bustling, cosmopolitan city after dark and tried to keep our presence—at first, anyway—a secret. But, as it usually happened, a friend told a friend in strictest confidence, who told *another* friend in strictest confidence, and soon even the sailors were hearing in the port that we were here as they disembarked from Africa, Gaul, and faraway Londinium!

That very night as we were eating, there was an urgent rapping on the door. When my host opened it, he found a woman in the doorway whose Syrian/Phoenician descent was obvious in spite of her Greek dress and manner.

"Please, kind sir," she begged our host, "take me to the Nazarene."

I silently motioned her in.

She stood before me and said, "Lord! Son of David, have mercy on me! My daughter is suffering terribly from demon-possession."

At the banqueting table, in addition to the twelve, were some of our host's closest friends. They were all Jews who lived in this country as though they were at home in Judea, having absorbed none of Phoenicia's cosmopolitan Hellenistic aura. It was obvious that they considered themselves much superior to this woman. They stared at her blankly, as if she were barely human.

I was so repulsed by their obvious disgust that I couldn't speak at first.

Then Judas spoke up. "Jesus, send her away, for she'll keep crying out after us if we don't."

Judas's words pained me, but I didn't let on at first. Instead, I told the woman, "I was sent only to the lost sheep of Israel."

The Gentile woman came and knelt before me. "Lord, help me as well."

I said, "Is it right to take the children's food and toss it to the dogs?"

She understood immediately what I was saying—even if my own people did not.

"Yes, Lord, of course that is not right. But even the dogs under the table are allowed to eat the children's crumbs."

She stared fiercely, proudly at me. But beneath her brave facade, her lower lip was trembling.

I smiled at her. *Would that my own people believed so strongly!*

"Woman, you have a great faith," I said. "For such a reply, you may go. The demon has left your daughter."

And, when she arrived back home, that is exactly what she found.

THE SIGN OF JONAH

Once again, the crush of the needy was so great that we found precious little peace in Tyre. After days of ceaseless healing and ministry, we straggled over to Sidon, Phoenicia's other large city—only to be met with the same overwhelming response.

The twelve were dragging. Petty disagreements were escalating into full-blown arguments. Even after everything we'd done, where once several families would offer to feed us in a village, we were struggling to find anyone who would house us even for a price.

And wherever we went, teams of Pharisees, led by Bald Pharisee and Goat-beard, preceded us, spreading their crafty rumors and outright lies.

So, as the summer wore on, we trudged across Phoenicia back toward the Sea of Galilee. Our goal was the Decapolis, the ten cities bunched on the eastern shore and south toward Perea. To avoid the Pharisees, however, we skirted Capernaum and went instead through Magdala, home of our friend Mary, who had faithfully been with us most of the previous year. But our enemies were lying in wait for us.

In Magdala, we were abruptly confronted by a gathering of Pharisees and Sadducees. The tension crackled in the late summer air as they trooped up. The haughty Sadducees proceeded to try and trap me. Their goal was to force me to prove my claims with a sign from heaven. The small crowd in attendance waited expectantly—the message I'd just spent the previous hours trying to explain utterly forgotten, lost forever.

I asked the Pharisees courteously, "May I first ask you a question? When evening comes, you say, 'It will be fair weather, for the sky is red,' and in the morning you say, 'Today it will be stormy, for the sky is red and overcast'—correct? All of you know how to interpret the appearance of the sky."

Yes, yes—they admitted that they all knew how to read the sky signs.

"But *none* of you know how to interpret the signs of the times!" I said angrily. "A wicked and adulterous generation looks for a miraculous sign, but none will be given it—except the sign of Jonah."

But it wasn't enough. Those in attendance began chanting for a sign as well, egged on by the Pharisees. I tried several times to continue my teaching but to no avail. After a few minutes, Mary led us away so that we could rest in peace.

THE YEAST OF THE PHARISEES

Early the following morning we set sail from Magdala for the Decapolis, hoping to have at least one uninterrupted meal en route. Once we were safely out of the harbor, Matthew turned to Andrew and Thaddaeus and said, "Okay boys, where's the bread and olive oil?"

Andrew jumped. "Uh, I got...busy, so I gave the money to Thaddaeus to get it for me."

Thaddaeus said, "That money was for breakfast today? I thought you just wanted me to hold it for safekeeping. I don't remember you saying anything about breakfast!"

"Thaddaeus, you simpleton," Andrew shouted, "I've got my own purse, I don't need you to keep my money for me. I very distinctly remember asking you to get the bread for breakfast with it."

They would have continued further, but I intervened.

"Be careful," I said. "Be on your guard against the yeast of the Pharisees and Sadducees."

I had other things on my mind than a few loaves of bread. But I heard Simon the Zealot turn to Andrew and say, "Whoo-wee! He's *really* mad about the breakfast!" The others nodded and edged away from me.

"O you of little faith," I said to all of them. "Are you still talking about the lost bread? Don't you understand? Don't you remember the five loaves that fed the five thousand—and how many baskets were left over? Or the other times we've fed the multitudes with virtually nothing? How is it that you *still* don't understand that I'm not talking about bread!?

"So let me tell you once again: *Be on your guard against the yeast of the Pharisees and Sadducees!*"

"Oh, I get it," John said brightly. "You weren't talking about baker's yeast—you were talking about the teachings of the Pharisees and Sadducees!"

"Yeah, and I guess we've been acting like them as well," Thaddaeus said. "I'm sorry I snapped at you, Andrew."

"I forgive you, Thaddaeus," he responded. "Now, can I have my money back?"

ON THIS ROCK I WILL BUILD MY CHURCH

In the hot, sticky days that followed, we worked our way through the cities of the Decapolis. We had some better success than we'd had on the western shore of the Sea of Galilee, and that reinvigorated us all. I wanted to hit the cities and villages north of Galilee before the weather turned cold again, so we headed toward Caesarea Philippi, by way of Bethsaida.

In Bethsaida, a group of friends and family members brought a blind man to me and begged me to touch him. I took the man by the hand and led him outside of the village. Then I spit on his eyes and placed my hands on him as he stood trembling before me.

"Do you see anything?" I asked.

"I...I see people," he whimpered. "They look like trees walking around—but I see them!"

I placed my hands over his eyes again.

"Now what do you see?"

"Everything!" he shouted, jumping up and down for joy.

"Good," I said. "Now, go home, but don't go through the heart of the village."

I'd heard that there were Pharisees prowling the streets looking for us, and there really wasn't time for a confrontation. Plus, something I didn't understand was urging me onward, northward.

So we continued north, stopping in each tiny village along the way. The sweet-spirited farmers and shepherds were gracious hosts and eager listeners. As we approached Caesarea Philippi, we found a stray stand of cedars and rested out of the early September sun. We'd left most of our followers behind as we'd traveled up the Jordan River—even our Pharisee watchdogs had left us for a time, though I had no doubt they were waiting for us in Caesarea Philippi.

So I turned to my disciples and asked, "Who do people say that the Son of Man is?"

Matthew said, "Some say John the Baptist returned. Others say Elijah. Some believe you are Jeremiah returned; still others have told us they believe you're one of the prophets."

I gathered them all closer. "But what about you? Who do *you* say that I am?"

Suddenly, Peter stood. "You are the Christ, the Son of the Living God!" He spoke with such a boldness that the others were shocked.

"Blessed are you, Simon Peter, son of Jonah," I said, "for this was not revealed to you by man, but by my Father in heaven. And I tell you that you are *Peter*, and on this rock I will build my church—and the gates of hell will not prevail against it! I will give you the keys of the kingdom of heaven. And whatever you bind on earth will be bound in heaven, and whatever you loose on earth will be loosed in heaven."

For once, all twelve seemed in agreement; for once they seemed to understand. A wave of contentment swept over me. But then the reality of our situation jarred me back.

"You must not tell anyone of this," I told them sternly. "The Son of Man must first suffer many things and be rejected by the elders, chief priests, and teachers of the law. And he must be killed and on the third day, be raised to life."

They all shot to their feet.

"No, Lord! No!" John shouted.

"This can't be right," Judas answered. "We will not allow it!"

I raised a hand for quiet.

"If anyone would come after me, he must deny himself and take up his cross daily and follow me. For whoever wants to save his life will lose it. But whoever loses his life for me will save it. Let me ask you: What good is it for a man to gain the whole world—and yet lose or forfeit his very self? If anyone is ashamed of me and my words, the Son of Man will be ashamed of him when he comes in his glory and in the glory of the Father and of the holy angels."

I dropped my voice to a barest whisper.

"In fact, some of you who are standing here will not taste death before you see the kingdom of God."

THE TRANSFIGURATION

Our ministry continued to take us generally northward. We worked and taught for a time in Caesarea Philippi, then slowly picked our way toward the Hermon mountain range, just northeast of town. Something about a certain mountain drew me unerringly. After about a week, I established a large camp at the foot of one of the mountains. Then I took Peter, James, and John with me as we scaled the summit. We approached the peak at late afternoon.

But with each step, I felt something happening to me. I couldn't explain it, but it was if I were filling up with light and love and peace. It was like the transcendent moment with dear John the Baptist in the River Jordan. My entire being was saturated with the love of my heavenly Father. I walked on eagle's wings; it seemed that I could go on forever. And as we scaled the summit, I began running like a deer, higher, further, sweeter, deeper.

The poor disciples struggled bravely behind me, huffing and puffing, working furiously to keep up.

But I reached the summit well before they did and felt that I could have continued running toward heaven. For the first time in—how long had it been?—I was alone. Alone!

It was a beautiful, breathtaking sight. I could see the Great Sea to the west, the Jordan, and the faintest glimmer of the Sea of Galilee to the south. At this elevation, the wind was cold and sharp, and it whipped my tunic and hair as I sat quietly, joyfully, soaking in the love.

At last, the three caught up with me, gasping for breath in the thin air.

Then it happened.

The divine entered the profane world below.

It entered ME.

No longer did visions flood into me, *the visions already within me were revealed.* What I had seen darkly in the Jordan and at Cana was now revealed to me in all of its brilliance.

Through the blinding light, I could see Peter, John, and James cowering around me, illuminated by a light brighter than all of the torches in Jerusalem. Great bolts of barely restrained light shot off in every direction, like Greek fire.

The light was warm and heavy around me, like sea water heated to body temperature. It was seeping into me, trickling in through every pore on my body.

When I looked up, I could see heaven.

I saw an endless stream of angels descending and ascending, floating on the light, laughing and chattering happily, singing glorious hymns, adding their light and love to the light emanating from my Father from the High Heaven beyond even my sight.

And then, drifting down through the angels were Moses and Elijah. They flanked me and we embraced as old friends, talking excitedly among us.

Distantly, as if underwater, I heard Peter shouting, "Lord, it is good for us to be here! If it's okay with you, I'd like to put up three booths—one for you, one for Moses, and one for Elijah. That is, if you don't mind or anything."

But then the light bloomed out like a cloud, enveloping all of us, cutting us off from the outside world. The angels suddenly stiffened and stopped, then bowed where they stood—or floated.

Then the most wonderful sound in the universe, my Father's unfathomable, unknowable, unmistakable voice filled us all to the cores of our very beings:

THIS IS MY SON, WHOM I LOVE; WITH HIM I AM WELL PLEASED. LISTEN TO HIM!

Peter, John, and Big James were bowled over by the impact of the voice. They lay cringing on the ground, burying their faces in the thin sand, shaking like leaves in a north wind.

Then the cloud, the light, Moses and Elijah, the singing, smiling angels, all disappeared.

I staggered slightly from the weight of the earth once again pulling on me. My head was filled with so many answers, I could scarcely sort them all out.

But the sight of my three friends whimpering in the dirt filled me with compassion. I walked over to them and said, "It's okay, you can get up now. Don't be afraid."

Big James peered up first, one eye darting between shaking fingers, looking wildly about. But only I stood there to greet him.

"Come, my friends," I said, "it is time for us to return."

I'm afraid I was lost in thought for much of the journey back to the camp. At last I was aware of the three watching me intently.

"Don't tell anyone what you've seen until the Son of Man has been raised from the dead," I cautioned them.

"But...but why?" Big James sputtered. "I mean, the whole world should know of this."

"No, don't you see?" John said quietly. "Jesus hasn't come as a conquering king like David, but as a religious leader—like Moses the lawgiver or Elijah the restorer of the prophetic order. We can't fuel this warrior/Messiah thing."

"Speaking of Elijah," Peter said, "why do the scribes and Pharisees say that Elijah must come first?"

"Actually," I answered, "Elijah *does* come first and restore all things. But Elijah *has* already come—and they didn't recognize him.

"In the same way," I continued sadly, "is the Son of Man going to suffer at their hands."

Peter's eyes widened as a light dawned within him.

"John the Baptist was Elijah," he said in a hushed whisper to the others. John and Big James nodded.

"Then," Peter continued, as if in a dream, "this is the Suffering Servant. Not on a white charger, not like Judas Maccabeus—but the Suffering Servant! *You* are the Suffering Servant that Isaiah and the others predicted would someday come!"

He was dumbfounded. The thought had never occurred to him before.

While Peter was musing, I was still assimilating everything that had been revealed to me. My soul shuddered in revulsion and fear when the three days following my...*death* were opened before me. I saw glimpses of gaping, hungry maws, of weird spider-like creatures skittering across a blasted landscape. I saw obscene parodies of all I held holy, bloated, grotesque images lumbering across the landscape, and nameless horrors and gibbering nightmares that walked on the souls of men. And, through it all, the piteously weeping face of Judas.

Is this what awaits me, Father?

I PROPHESY MY OWN DEATH

When our time there was complete, I reluctantly began moving south. Though the visions I had seen in the Hermons did not reveal every facet of my life to come, I had a strong sense that this might be the last time I see these windswept mountains.

As the summer began to wane, I felt a renewed urgency to share all I knew, all I believed, all I felt, with those loyal few who had followed me for so long.

Our first night in the more familiar foothills of Galilee, I called the twelve together. I wanted no confusion, no uncertainty about what I was about to say:

"The Son of Man is going to be betrayed into the hands of men. They will kill him and, on the third day, he will be raised to life again. Do you understand?"

Although I'd said this more than once before, I wasn't sure they *had* understood.

As the flames lit our faces, I stared unspeaking at the twelve, letting what I had said sink in.

No one spoke.

A few began crying silently, the tears glittering in the light of the fire.

This is good, I thought, *now we can finish this.*

But I misread their faces. Some of the twelve still did not understand.

PAYING TAXES

The remaining journey to Capernaum was completed over the next couple of days and I tried to teach the disciples the entire way. We stayed off the main road and avoided crowds so I could squeeze every spare minute for teaching. Since the harvest was in its early stages, few ventured to join us anyway.

Our collective reverie was shattered in Capernaum. Our old nemesis Goat-beard had arranged for a contingent of tax collectors to meet us at the gates. With a grim-faced retinue, the head tax collector folded his arms and blocked our way.

"Doesn't your teacher pay the temple tax?" he asked Peter.

Peter folded his arms and responded, "Why, yes, he does. Now, if you'll excuse us." He politely shouldered the man aside and we continued into the city.

Once at Maariah's house, we all reclined around an excellent meal—our first hot food in weeks.

After the blessing, I turned to Peter and said, "So, Simon Peter, what do you think? From whom do the kings of the earth collect duty and taxes—from their own sons or others?"

Peter gave me a quizzical look. "Well, from others, of course. Why?"

"Then the sons are exempt," I said.

Peter nodded.

But Matthew peered over his shoulder and out the open window. From his vantage point, he could see the tax collectors furiously checking their rolls.

"Uhhh, Master. *You* may know you're a son of the king, and *we* may know you're a son of the king—but *they* don't seem to know you're a son of the king. And they're about to cause a scene."

He was right. I looked back at Peter.

"So that we may not offend them," I said, "go to the lake and throw out a line. Take the first fish you catch and open its mouth. Inside you will find a four-drachma coin. Take it and give it to the tax collectors in payment for both my tax and yours."

Thaddaeus jumped up with Peter, grabbed his fishing pole, and headed for the door as well.

"Where are *you* going?" Matthew asked.

"To catch one of these four-drachma fish," he said. "I need a new tunic and my sandals could use new soles!"

WHO WILL BE THE GREATEST?

Maariah firmly kept the curious away for a few days while we all rested and gathered strength for the trials to come. I spent much of my time praying on the roof, out of sight of the onlookers below.

One morning I came down from my prayers and the twelve were milling around, talking quietly, but with plenty of animated gestures. I could tell they'd been arguing about something. I'd seen this look before.

"Say, this isn't the same discussion you guys had back on the road from Caesarea Philippi, is it?" I asked. "What was that all about?"

Everybody looked at the floor.

Bad sign.

"Okay," I sighed, "will someone tell me what this is all about?"

Finally, Andrew stepped forward, kicking imaginary rocks with his feet, still staring at the floor like a little boy.

"We, uh, have been, uh, debating, who is going to be, uh, greatest among us when we, uh, get to heaven."

This one caused me to rub my jaw for a moment and I sat down to think about it. At last I called for one of Peter's little nephews who was playing outside.

The boy bounded in and I had him stand in the midst of the fidgety disciples, then I hugged him tightly.

"If anyone wants to be first, he must be the very last," I said. "In fact, he must be the servant of all.

"In fact, whoever welcomes one of these little children in my name, welcomes me. And whoever welcomes me, not only welcomes me—but the One who sent me!"

John spoke up.

"This is probably a good time to ask this. While we were on our own, some of us saw a man driving out demons in your name."

"And what did you do?" I asked.

"Well, since he wasn't one of us," John said slowly, realizing how silly his words were suddenly sounding, "we, uh, told him to stop."

"Next time, don't stop him," I said. "No one who does a miracle in my name can—in the very next breath—say something bad about me. You see, whoever is not against us, is for us.

"And something else: Whoever gives you a cup of water in my name because you belong to Christ will certainly not lose his reward."

The little fellow I was holding was getting wiggly, eager to rejoin his pals outside.

"And finally, if anyone causes one of these little ones who believe in me to sin, it would be better for him to be thrown into the sea with a large millstone tied around his neck!

"See that you do not look down on one of these little ones. For I tell you that their angels in heaven always see the face of my Father in heaven."

I looked the little fellow in the eye.

"Okay, Little Master," I said, "I have a question for you. Say a man owns a hundred sheep and one of them wanders away. Does he stay with the remaining ninety-nine, or does he leave the ninety-nine and go search for the one that wandered off?"

The boy giggled.

"That's silly—he looks an' looks for the lost sheep—right?"

"Correct! And if he finds it, I know from personal experience that he is happier about that one sheep than about the ninety-nine that stayed put."

I looked back at the twelve.

"In the same way, your Father in heaven is not willing that any of these little ones be lost."

I gave the child one last squeeze. He impulsively turned, kissed me on the cheek, and broke free—laughing all the way out the door.

I watched him go for a minute, then unconsciously assumed what Nathanael called my "Serious Face"—meaning the teaching was about to be "difficult."

"My friends," I continued, "if your hand causes you to sin, cut it off. It is better for you to enter life maimed than with two hands—and go to hell where the fire never dies. And if your foot causes you to sin, cut it off. It is better for you to enter life crippled than to have two good feet and be thrown into hell. Finally, if your eye causes you to sin, pluck it out. I'm telling you that it is better for you to enter the kingdom of God with one eye than it would be to have two eyes and be tossed into hell where 'the worm does not die, and the fire is not quenched.'

"Everyone will be salted with fire. Sure, salt is good, but if it loses its saltiness—how can you make it salty again? You can't. Have salt in yourselves, and be at peace with each other."

The twelve looked sheepishly at each other.

For once, I think I've hit the mark. Maybe this'll put an end to that silly business about who is going to sit at my right hand!

How Many Times Shall I Forgive?

Now, let's go see if there is anyone in this sleepy little fishing village whom the Pharisees haven't turned against us!"

We wandered over to the early morning market, already noisy with the cries of fishmongers, tent-makers, jewelers, farmers, and shoppers. I smelled saffron, curry, and fresh goat cheese—and even fresher fish. I enjoyed the good-natured haggling and bantering of merchants. And I liked the anonymity I could sometimes find in a busy market.

At last, we found a sunny corner and I began to talk and ask questions of the twelve. Soon, a small crowd joined them.

"If we're lucky, maybe ol' Bald Pharisee will be in the synagogue all day," Matthew muttered, "and we can get some serious teaching done!"

In time, our discussion turned to forgiveness.

"If your brother sins against you, go and show him his fault—just between the two of you," I said. "If he listens to you, you have won your brother over. But if not, take a couple of others along so that every matter may be established by the testimony of two or three witnesses."

"What if he refuses to listen to them?" Simon asked.

"Then tell it to the assembly," I answered. "And if he *still* refuses to listen even to the assembly, then treat him as you would a pagan or..."

I paused dramatically.

"...a tax collector!"

The other eleven hooted at Matthew's expense, who forced a weak smile.

"Like I've said before: That if two or three of you agree about anything you ask for, it will be done for you by my Father in heaven. For where two or three come together in my name, there am I with them."

Again, it was Peter who asked the telling question.

"Lord, how many times shall I forgive my brother when he sins against me? Take Goat-beard, for instance. Shall I forgive him seven times?"

"No, Peter, what I'm telling you is that you should forgive him not seven times—but seventy-seven times!"

Judas spit in the dirt in disgust. Like Peter, he still had scars from previous encounters with Goat-beard and Bald Pharisee and their men.

"Let me put it this way," I said. "The kingdom of heaven is like a king who wanted to settle accounts with his servants. As he began the settlement, a servant who owed him the unthinkable amount of ten thousand talents was brought to him. Since he was obviously unable to pay, the master ordered that he and his wife and children—and all that he had—be sold to repay the debt.

"But the servant groveled before his master and begged, 'Master, please be patient with me. Give me time—I will pay back everything! I swear!'

"The master took pity on the man and his family and said, 'Oh, okay. Your debt is canceled.'

"Overjoyed, the servant and his family left the king's palace. But just outside the door, he encountered a fellow servant who owed *him* a trifling hundred denarii. The first servant grabbed the second by the throat and began choking him. 'Pay back what you owe me, you wretch! Now!'

"But the second servant fell to his knees and whimpered, 'Be patient with me, friend—and I will pay you back as soon as I possibly can.'

"But the first servant refused. 'Not good enough!' he howled. Enraged, he had the poor man thrown into prison until the debt was paid!

"Well, the other servants saw the first servant's hideous treatment of the poor man and ran and told the king everything that happened.

"The king called the first servant back before him. 'You wicked servant!' he shouted. 'I canceled all that huge debt of yours because you begged me to. You should have had mercy on your fellow servant—just as I had mercy on your worthless hide!'

"Now the king was *really* angry. He turned the first servant over to the jailers to be tortured until he could pay back everything he owed!"

I have their attention now! I thought.

"This is how my heavenly Father will treat each of you unless you forgive your brother from your heart."

Just then, Andrew saw Bald Pharisee and his handpicked gang storming our way, overturning stalls and scattering chickens before them, itching for a fight.

"Oh, brother!" Andrew said with an exasperated sigh. "It's time to forgive ol' Baldie for the 453rd time!"

And it was.

My Brother Embarassed

Despite the opposition, we continued to minister and teach throughout Galilee for as long as possible. The nights were turning cooler, and I was beginning to feel a strange urgency about my ministry here.

We were in the vicinity of Nazareth one afternoon when my brothers, James, Judas, Simon, and Joseph, tracked me down. Joseph took me aside and said, "Jesus, you really ought to leave here and go to Judea, you know. This way your disciples there may see the miracles you do. No one who wants to become a public figure acts in secret. Since you're doing these miracles anyway, show the world!"

It was obvious from his words that Joseph didn't believe me. I think Judas, Simon, and Joseph were urging me to go to Jerusalem so I wouldn't keep embarrassing them in Nazareth. Strangely, James was silent. He couldn't look me in the eye, either. Something was happening in his life as well.

I told Joseph, "The time's not right for me to go publicly to Jerusalem. For you, any time's right. You're not the one the world hates because you're not the one saying what the world is doing is evil. But you four go on ahead."

"Well, I'm glad *that's* settled," Simon the Zealot said. "There's no way I could guarantee your safety in Jerusalem."

"Oh, I'm going to the Feast of Booths, all right," I said. "But not in public."

Simon helplessly threw up his hands.

"Honestly, Jesus—I don't know what we're going to do with you."

You've spoken few words more true than these, dear Simon, I thought sadly.

CHAPTER FIVE

Jerusalem—The Sign of Jonah

AN ENCOUNTER IN SAMARIA

So we departed the next day heading south, although I told only the original twelve about my plans to slip into Jerusalem for the Feast. More than a hundred of my most devoted followers joined us by the time we left Capernaum. Despite ferocious opposition, there were still many who believed and followed. The women in particular were not cowed by the Pharisees' veiled threats and outright intimidation. But our final hours in the city were filled with nonstop oppression and outright abuse.

We had barely left the city limits of Capernaum when a man came running up and breathlessly said, "I will follow you, Lord! But first let me say good-bye to my family."

But I could see his heart. "No one who puts his hand to the plow and looks back is fit for service in the kingdom of God."

With that, the man drifted away.

Strangely enough, the farther south we traveled, the greater the fervor among my disciples. Some, like Peter and John, were just glowing with the Holy Spirit, eager to learn, eager to teach, eager to do great works in my name.

As was his custom, Matthew meticulously sent runners ahead to each village, to ensure that there was enough food available to feed our followers and—if necessary—secure lodging for the evening.

As we walked through northern Samaria, he again sent two men ahead to the nearest town, Salim. The twelve were anxious to return to Samaria; we'd enjoyed some of our greatest successes there.

To my surprise, we were met at Salim's city gates by an armed contingent of Samaritans.

"A party of a hundred Jews heading for Jerusalem—through Salim?!" the elder said incredulously. "What mischief is this? This many Jews in one place can only mean trouble."

"Please, if you'll give us a moment to explain," Peter said.

A couple dozen men stepped forward, pulled swords from their scabbards, pointed spears, and brandished pitchforks in our direction.

"Explain all you want, Jew!" the elder said. "But do it when you're a mile further down the road. Another step and we'll kill the lot of you!"

Still, Big James and John boldly tried to reason with them, telling the elders how we'd been received earlier in Samaria. But on a signal from the elder, some of the Samaritan young men slapped the two around, then forcibly threw them out of the gates.

Big James painfully rubbed his backside, shook a fist at the jeering mob, and said, "Lord, do you want us to call fire down from heaven to destroy this perverse city?"

"No, leave them be," I said. "We will cross the Jordan and continue our journey on the eastern shore of the river, out of Samaritan lands."

"But why didn't you smite them, Rabbi?" Simon asked, genuinely confused.

"Because these people have good reason to fear and mistrust Jews," Nathanael said. "If you've been persecuted for centuries, wouldn't *you* be a trifle testy if a mob of Jews wanted to troop through your town?"

Well said, Nathanael!

SENDING THE SEVENTY-TWO

Fortunately, the incident in Samaria did little to dampen the high spirits of those in the traveling party. In northern Judea, I found the village of Bethabara welcoming and hospitable, so I called a meeting of my followers.

"I'm going to send you out ahead of me in groups of two, to every village and town in Perea, the Decapolis, and Judea," I said. "The harvest is plentiful, but the workers are few. So ask the Lord of the Harvest to send more workers. Now go! I am sending you out like lambs among the wolves."

Then I told them again what was expected of them, how they were to behave, what they could take, where they should go.

"Shall we send someone to Korazin or Bethsaida, Lord?" asked Matthew.

I flinched at the mention. Both cities had seen numerous miracles and had yet continually rejected and despised our message.

"Woe to Korazin and Bethsaida!" I said. "You know, if the miracles we had performed there had been performed in Tyre and Sidon, those towns would have repented long ago, and the entire population would be in the streets, sitting in sackcloths, covered with ashes. I'm afraid it will be more bearable for Tyre and Sidon on the Judgment Day than it will be for Korazin and Bethsaida."

"What of Capernaum?" Peter asked slowly. "Shall we send two there?"

Our final days in Capernaum had been a nightmare, hounded and harassed by mobs employed by the Pharisees, our followers driven underground, poor Maariah forced to barricade her doors and windows at night.

"I'm sorry, Peter," I said, "Capernaum will not be lifted up to the skies on that day. Instead, it will be crushed to the depths. But yes—we will send two there as well.

"He who listens to you, listens to me. He who rejects you, rejects me. But remember this: he who rejects me, rejects him who sent me."

Then I sent the seventy-two on their way, men and women, young and old, and they fanned out across the land, joyfully, boldly proclaiming the Good News.

THE SEVENTY-TWO RETURN

I remained in Bethabara, near where John had originally baptized me, praying and gathering my strength for the storm to come. I stayed at the large, ramshackle home of Zaccur. He was a loyal friend. His house would become a well-known refuge for us in times of trial—and many of our followers would find their way here in the days ahead.

And, over the next few weeks, they returned, filtering back across deserts, over mountains, through swollen rivers, all heading back to Bethabara. They returned singing and dancing with joy, flushed with the power of the Holy Spirit.

Peter must have run the last few miles. He arrived flushed and sweating profusely, his eyes blazing with holy fire.

"Lord! Even the demons submitted to us in your name!"

He grabbed me in a massive bearhug, dancing in little circles. Others, trailing close behind Peter, told similar stories.

After they'd had time to catch their breath, we sat in a tight circle. While they'd been gone, I'd been remembering what had come…before. I wanted to share these memories while they were still fresh.

"I saw Satan fall like lightning from heaven," I told them slowly, remembering that awful day.

It will be forever scorched in my mind's eye like a torturers' brand. There, at the foot of the throne that stretches a thousand miles, preening and pouting, stood Lucifer, the most beautiful, most powerful of the angels. I stood in horror, transfixed by the cosmic blasphemy unfolding before me. Massed around Lucifer was his army of followers, alternately egging him on and fawning before him.

I had to restrain Gabriel and Michael from plowing into their seemingly endless ranks. They flanked me, shaking with revulsion and rage over the profanity.

And then, the smallest, most basic components of creation exploded.

The backlash shook the very foundations of heaven.

And Lucifer was gone.

Forever.

And I cried for him and those lost angels who chose to follow him.

And my Father cries still.

"Uh, Master, you were saying?" Thomas said tentatively.

"Sorry, I was…remembering," I said.

I scanned the small group assembled before me, each with miraculous stories to tell.

"I have given you authority to trample on snakes and scorpions. I have given you the power to overcome the Enemy. *Nothing* will harm you.

"However, do not rejoice that the evil spirits submit to you. Instead, rejoice that your names are written in heaven."

In the hours that followed, the rest of the seventy-two returned to Zaccur's house with similar stories of power and faith. They eagerly shared their experiences with each other and praised God for their friends' successes.

Shortly before it was time to retire for the evening, I called everyone together for a mass meeting and prayer session. I ended with this prayer:

"I praise you Father, Lord of heaven and earth, because you have hidden these things from the wise and the learned and instead revealed them to little children!"

Then, after we'd dismissed, I gathered the twelve privately and said, "Blessed are the eyes that see what you see. For I'm telling you that a host of kings and prophets would have given their fortunes to see the miracles you've seen and heard. Remember these days always."

AN ANGRY MOB

Early the next morning, I sent many of the seventy-two back to their homes, to continue preaching the message I'd given them.

I took a much smaller contingent into Jerusalem. We skirted the walls and entered through the less obvious Gennath Gate and tried to blend in with the masses surging through the streets to celebrate the Feast of Booths.

Everywhere we went, we heard people asking, "Will Jesus of Nazareth be here?" Some would respond, "Oh, I hope so! He is a good man, a healer, a miracle-maker." Others would say, "No! The Pharisees and Sadducees say he is a false prophet, one who will bring down the wrath of Rome on our heads!"

When the Feast was half over, I felt compelled to go to the Temple courts and teach. Simon and Judas made halfhearted efforts to dissuade me and instead resigned themselves to forming a loose perimeter around me for defensive purposes. I would have asked them not to, but it made them feel useful.

The teaching went well. Soon I was enjoying a vigorous question-and-answer session with a number of learned men and a healthy crowd gathered. I don't think anyone recognized me at first.

At last, a Pharisee in a bright blue robe stepped forward. "How did you get such learning without having studied?" he asked.

"My teaching is not my own," I said. "It comes from him who sent me. If anyone chooses to do God's will, he will find out whether my teaching comes from God or whether I speak on my own.

"Usually, someone who speaks on his own is only doing so to gain fame and honor. But the man who works for the glory of the One who sent me is a man of truth.

"Has not Moses given you the law? Yet not one of you keeps the law. So…"

I paused briefly, staring into Blue Robe's eyes.

"…why are *you* trying to kill me?"

Blue Robe jumped back as if bitten by a snake. He looked wildly about the crowd for his friends. "You're crazy! Or maybe you're just demon-possessed. *Who* is trying to kill you?"

My eyes never left his.

"I did one miracle and you are all astonished. Yet, because Moses gave you circumcision—though actually it did not come from Moses but from the patriarchs—you circumcise a child on the Sabbath. Now, if a child can be circumcised on the Sabbath so that no law of Moses may be broken—why are you angry with me for healing a man on the Sabbath? Stop judging me by appearances! Make a right judgment!"

A murmur shot through the crowd and I heard the babble of dozens of excited voices: "It's him! It's Jesus of Nazareth!" "He's the one who healed the lame man by the pool!" "Isn't he the one the authorities are trying to kill?" "Have they really admitted that he's the Christ?" "But I thought the prophets said *no one* would know where the Christ comes from."

And so it went, each man talking rapidly to the man next to him. Somebody roughly cuffed Blue Robe from behind and he

whirled and glared into the crowd. I saw Simon nervously fingering his dagger.

Simon has good instincts about a crowd's mood, I thought.

Sure enough, in a few seconds, the questions turned mean-spir-
ited and confrontational. It appeared that Blue Robe and his
friends were at the bottom of it.

"Yes, you know me and you know where I am from," I shouted over the tumult. "But then you should also know that I am
not here of my own accord. You should know that he who sent
me is always true, always steadfast. I'm afraid many of you do not
know him. But please hear me: it was he who sent me. I am from
him!"

It was no use. With a roar, the mob overwhelmed my thin line
of disciples and grabbed me. In the blinking of an eye, I saw a
dozen assassin's daggers exposed and flashing toward me.

It was as if time itself slowed to a crawl: the silver rain of daggers floating toward my heart, the twisted faces full of hate
behind them, screaming obscenities and spewing venom, Simon
and Peter howling in frustration, held back by a hundred hands,
a maddening roar filling all of our ears.

"Enough," I said simply. And it was.

"It is not yet my time."

And with the knives still poised in mid-strike, like silver fin-
gerlings in a fast-rushing creek, I walked between my would-be
assassins and back out into the Temple grounds.

As the Pharisees and their bullies stood momentarily transfixed, a large portion of the crowd followed me, eager to learn—
and believe.

One man turned to Little James and said, "When the Christ
actually comes, how will he accomplish more miracles than this
man? He's amazing!"

Little James had to laugh.

But others voiced similar sentiments in the presence of other Pharisees, who promptly found the chief priests. Simon tagged along, pretending to be another concerned citizen.

"It's blasphemy of the highest order!" Blue Robe fumed. "The man is making a mockery of this holy place! He's a charlatan. And worse, he's a dangerous charlatan."

"Exactly so," one of the chief priests responded. "What if Rome should hear that we can't police our own? They might...we might lose our positions!"

According to Simon, *that* little observation galvanized the priests. They immediately sent the Temple guards to arrest me. Simon raced ahead and found me still speaking with those of the crowd who had followed me.

"They're coming to arrest you, Master!" he cried.

I could see the armed guards pouring from the Temple portals, marching toward us.

"I am with you for only a short time," I told my followers, "and then I go back to the One who sent me. You will look for me, but you will not find me. For where I am, you cannot follow."

This confused more than one of my listeners.

"What's that mean, Teacher?" one man asked. "Where is this place you will go that we can't follow? Will you go stay with our people who live scattered among the Greeks—and teach the Greeks?"

But with the guards now in a dead run, there was no time to explain. We melted in all directions into the larger crowd milling obliviously around us.

"HE HAS OPENED MY EYES"

We stayed in Jerusalem a few more days, letting things cool down. When I did make forays out to preach, I stayed away from the Temple, speaking only to small groups. Or, I took the disciples on short tours of the ancient city, teaching as we went, presenting only a moving target to my growing list of enemies.

One afternoon, we were deep in discourse when we passed a blind man—and they were legion in Jerusalem. My disciples took a clinical approach, regarding the poor man like an object lesson.

"Rabbi," Judas asked, "who sinned, this man or his parents, for him to have been blind?"

I was hurt that they would talk about the blind man within his hearing as if he were deaf as well, so I responded immediately: "Actually, neither he nor his parents sinned. He was born blind so that the works of God might be displayed in him."

My unseeing disciples—sometimes I think YOU are the blind men. Sometimes I think YOU are the ones who are truly deaf. You haven't been paying attention to ANYTHING I've said, have you?

I was so exasperated, I stopped the procession by the blind man and said, "As long as the day lasts, I must carry out the work of the One who sent me—for the night will soon be here when no one can work. As long as I am in the world, I am the light of the world."

And, as usual, no one understood.

So I spit into the dusty ground, made a mud pie, placed it over the eyes of the startled blind man, then sent him, accompanied by John, to the nearby Pool of Siloam, which is at the foot of the hill of the old City of David—just south of the Temple area.

John told us later that the man complied. And when he washed off the mud, he could see!

The man was surrounded by his neighbors, who didn't recognize him until he insisted he was the same formerly blind beggar who sat by the Temple.

"Who healed you?" they asked.

"The man called Jesus," he responded, gazing in wonder at the blue Judean sky that he was seeing for the first time.

But John said he was immediately dragged before the Pharisees, some of the same Pharisees who—only days before—had tried to stone me in the Temple. Led by—you guessed it—Goat-beard. Some of the Pharisees were dumbfounded, others were angered when the man told them that it was I who healed him.

"This man cannot be from God; he does not keep the Sabbath!" Goat-beard snarled at the man—evidently in reference to my mixing the water and clay to make mud on a Sabbath!

But John said that the healed man was adamant in his assertion: "He is a prophet. Sabbath or Wednesday—what does it matter? I can see!"

The Pharisees then sent for his parents. John told us that they quickly vouched for him.

"We know he is our son and we know he was born blind," they said upon arriving.

But John said he could see their joy turning into fear. The Pharisees crowded around them, muttering darkly. He heard a few implied threats, perhaps even expulsion from the Temple.

Visibly shaken, the man's parents weakly protested to the Pharisees, "But we don't know how it is that he can see now, or who opened his eyes. He is old enough: let him speak for himself!"

The formerly blind man again stood confidently before them. John reported to us that the Pharisees tried to bully him into changing his story, but he bravely resisted their efforts to brand me a sinner.

Then, when they repeated their earlier questions, his tone changed from exasperation to sarcasm: "I have told you once and you wouldn't listen. Why do you want to hear it all again? Do you want to become his disciples too?"

John said that the crowd that had now gathered to hear the impromptu debate chuckled at the Pharisees' discomfort.

After conferring among themselves, John said Goat-beard spit out their response: "You poor, misguided simpleton! You can follow whoever you like, but *we* will remain true believers, the unsullied followers of Moses and the One True God—not some itinerant homeless teacher from Galilee!"

But the man, who was once blind and now could see clearly, would not be so easily dismissed. John had to laugh over his retort: "Now here is an astonishing thing! He has opened my eyes, and you don't know where he comes from! We know that God doesn't listen to sinners, but God does listen to men who are devout and do his will. Ever since the world began, it is unheard of for anyone to open the eyes of a man born blind. So, if this man is not from God, he couldn't do a thing. Right?"

Obviously, that man had done more than just beg at the Temple gates—he had been a keen participant in the sighted world that swirled past him every day.

John told us that the assembled crowd roared with laughter as the enraged Pharisees sent him away, his still-whimpering parents cowering in his wake.

Moments later, just outside of the Temple walls, he walked up—still accompanied by John.

"Do you believe in the Son of Man?" I asked him warmly.

The once-blind man recognized my voice and without hesitation said, "Sir, tell me who he is so that I may believe in him."

"You are looking at him, my friend; he is speaking to you."

Immediately, the man fell at my feet and cried, "Lord, I believe."

WINTER IN BETHANY

But after that incident, Goat-beard and his cohorts began closing the net tighter. It became harder and harder to find—and keep—lodging. The Temple guards redoubled their efforts to keep us away from the sprawling Temple complex. Bands of paid thugs hounded us mercilessly. And when we could speak, our audiences were conspicuously smaller.

So we moved our base of operations to the home of Mary, Martha, and Lazarus in Bethany, just a short two-mile walk east of Jerusalem. The three were some of our oldest and most devoted friends and time spent with them was precious beyond measure.

As the winter moved in, we spent our nights in Bethany, coming into Jerusalem on an erratic and ever-changing schedule. We avoided the Temple and stuck to isolated corners in Jerusalem, preaching for a day, then pulling out. Simon and Judas loved it. Simon called it "guerilla evangelism," and Judas said it reminded him of the hit-and-run tactics of his beloved Maccabbees.

The main Roman road from Bethany to Jerusalem turns north in the Kidron Valley, just east of the city, and leads directly into the Temple portico, near the Pool of Israel. In time, we realized that that route was no longer safe, so we instead turned south in the Kidron Valley within sight of the city walls. Our plan was to take the old paths to the southernmost gate of the Lower City, called the Water Gate.

One cold morning, after preaching elsewhere in Judea and Perea for several weeks, we returned to Jerusalem via this southern route. As we passed the Spring Gihon and Hezekiah's Tunnel, our blood froze.

On the heights overlooking the valley stood a dozen crosses bearing rotted corpses. Carrion birds picked halfheartedly at the few remaining shards of flesh, and the skulls stared at us with blind death's-head grins. Their alleged crimes were written above their heads, but were already too faded for us to read.

I have seen crosses like these in my visions.

And I am on one of those crosses.

John must have seen the look of horror that crossed my face.

"What is it, Lord?"

"Pray for the souls of those poor wretches, my friend," I said, my voice a husky whisper.

"I shall, Lord. And I shall pray that I do not die hanging from a Roman cross."

"I will pray for that as well, John."

Judas caught up with us, his voice barely disguising his hatred of Rome.

"As a boy, I once saw more than a thousand such crosses outside Jerusalem," he said, never taking his eyes off the road ahead of us. "They were the victims of some rebellion or another. Our Roman 'guests' crucified entire families. A few blasted souls lasted a week or more in the broiling sun, their bodies parboiled into hellish blisters, croaking for the mercy of a quick death. I never forgot the sight. From a distance, it looked like a small city. Until the wind changed."

We walked the rest of the way in abject, brooding silence.

THE GOOD SAMARITAN

Once inside the Water Gate, Matthew found a sympathetic rabbi and his school near the Hippodrome. The rabbi's name was Malkijah and soon we were engaged in a spirited debate.

It quickly became apparent that Malkijah liked the feeling of authority—and didn't like for anyone else to shine in his students' eyes. I was about to end the debate when he decided to test me, perhaps to regain some lost stature with his pupils.

"Teacher," he said grandly, "what must I do to inherit eternal life?" He then sat down and made a great show of listening intently. It was painfully obvious that this was one subject he'd studied extensively.

"First, may I ask you a question, Malkijah?"

"Of course."

"What is written in the Law? How do *you* read it?"

"Why, the Law says 'Love the Lord your God with all your heart and with all your soul and with all your strength and with all your mind.' It also says, 'Love your neighbor as yourself.'"

I bowed slightly. "You have, of course, answered correctly. Do this and you will live."

I moved to withdraw, but Malkijah was not through with me yet. John sighed over-loudly; we'd seen this self-aggrandizing behavior all too often.

"One last question, Teacher: and just who *is* my neighbor?"

"Perhaps you'll forgive me if I answer with one last story," I said as courteously as I knew how. Malkijah nodded and expertly spread his hands, palms outward.

"A man was traveling from Jerusalem to Jericho when he was savagely attacked by bandits. They beat him mercilessly, stripped him of his clothes, and stole all that he owned—leaving him for dead on the road.

"A few minutes later, a priest came down that same road. He saw the man lying in a pool of blood, delicately crossed to the other side of the road, and continued on his way. Shortly after that, a Levite came riding down the same road and saw the half-dead man. He too passed by on the other side of the road.

"Finally, a Samaritan rode up. He saw the poor man and his heart was filled with pity. He bandaged the man's wounds as best he could, tenderly lifted him on to his own donkey, and took him to the nearest inn. Once there, the Samaritan cared for him throughout the night, even pouring oil and wine onto his wounds. "And when morning came, the Samaritan found the innkeeper, pressed two silver coins into his hands, and said, 'Please look after this poor soul. And when I return, I will reimburse you for any additional expenses you may have incurred on his behalf.'"

I smiled at Malkijah. "Which of these three men do *you* think was the neighbor of the man beaten by robbers?"

Malkijah stuttered and stammered a moment, then said, "Well, from this *particular* set of *extreme* and *highly unlikely* circumstances, I think the *typical* student of the Law would *most likely* agree with me that the…uh…Samaritan was, indeed, the unfortunate man's neighbor."

A few of my disciples snickered, but I kept smiling at poor, flustered Malkijah. "Go and do likewise," I said.

Malkijah suddenly remembered a pressing appointment, dismissed his class, and we never saw him again.

THE LORD'S PRAYER

But others had heard the exchange and our largest crowd in days settled in all around us. Judas and Simon took their customary positions at the nearest street corners, watching for the Pharisees and their bully-boys, and I found a large stone fence to sit on.

The discussion turned to prayer. Eventually, Andrew raised his hand to speak. "Lord, teach us to pray—just as John the Baptizer taught Peter and me to pray when we were his disciples."

"A fair request, Andrew," I said. "When you pray, say 'Father in heaven, holy be your name. May your kingdom come, your will be done—on earth as it is in heaven. Please give us each day our daily bread. Please forgive our debts even as we forgive our debtors. Please lead us not into temptation. And please deliver us from the Evil One. For yours is the power and the glory forever. Amen.' "

One of those listening in the audience said, "I've never heard a prayer like that, Rabbi. I'm not sure what it means."

"Think of it this way," I said. "Suppose Nathanael has a friend..."

"I don't believe this story already!" Thomas snickered.

"...who suddenly appears at his door at midnight..."

"If you're a friend of Nathanael's, that's the *only* time you go see him and not be embarrassed!" Peter hooted.

Before Nathanael could retort, I cocked an eyebrow at all of them.

"If you'll forgive the intrusion, I'd like to respond to the gentleman's comment," I said, being careful to look severe.

"Suppose Nathanael has a friend who suddenly appears at his door at midnight," I continued. "The friend says, 'Nathanael, lend me three loaves of bread because a friend on a long journey has unexpectedly come to me and I have nothing to set before him.' "

"Nathanael will shout from his bedroom, 'Go away—don't bother me! The door is already locked and my children are already in bed. I can't get up and get you anything.'

"But in time Nathanael *will* get up. Not because this man is a friend, but because of his friend's persistence. He'll keep knocking on the door, asking for bread, until Nathanael is forced to get out of bed to get any sleep.

"So, I say to you, ask and it will be given to you. Seek and you will find. Knock and the door will be opened to you. Everyone who asks, receives. Everyone who seeks, finds. And everyone who knocks, will see the door opened.

"Or think of it this way: If your son asks you for a fish, which of you fathers will give him a snake, instead? If your son asks for an egg, which of you will give him a scorpion? Even wicked men know how to give gifts to their children. How much more will your Father in heaven give the Holy Spirit to those who ask?"

THE SIGN OF JONAH—AGAIN

But I hadn't mollified everybody. "A sign! How about a sign!" came yet another muffled voice from the crowd.

I slumped wearily on the old stone fence.

"This is a wicked generation," I said flatly. "It asks for a miraculous sign, but none will be given—except the sign of Jonah."

"And what is this so-called 'sign of Jonah' you keep mentioning?" the same voice hissed. I saw Simon angrily scanning the crowd, looking for the source, but there were simply too many people.

"As Jonah was a sign to the Ninevites, so also will the Son of Man be a sign to this generation," I said. "The Queen of the South will rise at the judgment with the men of this generation and condemn them—for she came from the ends of the earth to listen to Solomon. And now, one greater than Solomon is here.

"The men of Nineveh will stand up at the judgment with this generation and condemn it—for they repented at the preaching of Jonah. And now, one greater than Jonah is here."

At that moment, my heart skipped a beat. Blue Robe! I saw Blue Robe, his face half-hidden in shadow by his hood, trying to blend in to the middle of the crowd. I focused my attention on him.

"No one lights a lamp and puts it in a place where it will be hidden," I said, carefully measuring my words. "Instead, he puts it on its stand, so that those who come in may see the light. Your eyes are the lamps of your body, my friends. When your eyes are good, your whole body also is full of light. But when they are bad, your body is full of darkness.

"See to it then that the light within you is not darkness. So, if your whole body is full of light and nothing in it is dark, it will be completely lighted—as when the light of a lamp shines on you."

DINNER WITH BLUE ROBE

With that, the crowd began breaking up. It was close to lunchtime and the cold wind had begun picking up. Soon, only a few people were still standing around, talking with the disciples. One of them was Blue Robe. He looked about nervously and said, "Uh, Teacher, why don't you and your disciples, uh, come and dine with me. Perhaps there is something we can...learn from one another."

Judas was so surprised, he dropped our money bag!

But I agreed.

Something is working on this man's heart.

Blue Robe's real name was Makir and he was a wealthy, influential Pharisee with a sprawling house in the Greek manner. While waiting for our food, we reclined around his tables. I especially enjoyed the conversation with Gamaliel, one of the greatest of all rabbis in Jerusalem.

"Ah, Gamaliel, your reputation for common sense and balanced liberality is well founded," I said, shortly before the food arrived.

"And you are wise beyond your years, Jesus of Nazareth," he said. "I have a student you simply must meet. He is a Roman citizen, reared in the university town of Cilicia, extraordinarily well educated—but his heart burns with a fire for the faith of our fathers."

"I would enjoy meeting such a man. What is his name?"

"Saul."

Just then, the food arrived and I joined my disciples in eating.

But Makir shot to his feet, his handsome face contorted in confused anger.

"But...but you have not first ceremonially washed! How could you do this to me—in my own household!"

The other Pharisees jumped to their feet, muttering "Unclean! Unclean!"—all save Gamaliel, who intently watched the drama unfolding before him.

For the Pharisees—and my disciples—the pleasant meal was ruined.

"You Pharisees clean the outside of the cup and dish, but inside you are full of greed and wickedness," I said. "You foolish people! The One who made the outside makes the inside as well! You should instead give what is inside the dish to the poor and everything will be clean for you."

"This is an interesting concept you propose, Jesus," Gamaliel said. "What exactly have the Pharisees done?"

"First, you Pharisees give God a tenth of your mint, rue, and all other kinds of garden herbs—but you neglect justice and the love of God. You should have practiced the latter without leaving the former undone.

"Second, you love the most important seats in the synagogues and greetings in the marketplaces.

"And third, you are like unmarked graves, which men walk over without knowing it."

Makir knotted up his fists. "How dare you! Alone of my friends, I tried to listen to you with an open mind. Alone of my friends, I dared invite you to my home. And this is how you repay my hospitality—by insulting me?"

I rose to leave.

"Makir, for once, listen to me with your mind, not your emotions. Many Pharisees and lawyers—not all, but many—load our people down with burdens they can hardly carry, but you yourselves will not lift one finger to help them.

"You build tombs for the prophets—but it was your forefathers who killed them. Don't you see that by doing this, you are tacitly approving of what your fathers did? God said you'd do this over and over in the books of the Law and Prophets— and you have!

"As a result, this generation will be responsible for the blood of all the prophets that has been shed since the dawn of time, from the blood of Abel to the blood of Zechariah—who was killed between the altar and sanctuary.

"And finally, you experts in the law will be held accountable because you have taken away the key to knowledge. You yourselves have not entered—and yet you continue to hinder those who were trying to enter.

"Makir, you know all of this is true. Pray about it, my friend, listen for God's guiding. He will show you the way to go."

I reached a hand for Makir's shoulder, but he roughly knocked it away.

I reluctantly left, my still-hungry disciples trailing behind me.

As soon as Simon was out the door, the room erupted in shouting. I could hear their curses and threats. My time in Jerusalem was growing short.

But when I looked back over my shoulder, I could see Gamaliel staring at us through the window.

MARY AND MARTHA

When we returned to Bethany, cold and starving, we were met by a roaring fire, warm hugs, and ready smiles from Mary,

Martha, Lazarus, and their servants. We collapsed by the fire and began to rehash the events and the teachings of the day. Mary sat by my feet, listening intently to what was being said.

Meanwhile, poor Martha was bustling about the house, barking orders, stirring pots in the kitchen, trying to cook enough food for all of us.

At last, exasperated, she came storming into the den, furiously wiping her hands on her apron.

"Lord," she said, "don't you care that my sister has left me to do all of the work by myself? Tell her to help me!"

"Martha, Martha," I said lovingly, "you are worried and upset by many things—but, for the moment, only one thing is needed. Mary has chosen what is better for her and it will not be taken away from her."

Martha frowned a moment, then plopped on the floor beside the Nathanael.

"Why beat them when you can join them?" she sighed.

TEACHING IN JERICHO

Outside, the cold north wind slammed harmlessly against the thick stone of the house of Mary, Martha, and Lazarus.

Once the storm had blown past, we left after a few days and headed east, through the rugged Judean wilderness, toward Jericho. Just south of Jericho was the brooding fortress of Cyprus, a few miles further south, the Dead Sea, and the mysterious Qumran community, once John the Baptizer's home.

The people in Jericho hadn't been tainted by Pharisee and Herodian lies and so were, for the most part, eager to hear our message. At one point, the crowd grew so large that I feared someone might be trampled. I asked some of our friends, including Lazarus, to arrange them in some kind of order, so I might speak. While they were doing so, I spoke privately with the twelve.

"Once again, be on guard against the yeast of the Pharisees," I said. "Many of them are hypocrites. Believe me: there is nothing concealed that will not be eventually disclosed, nothing hidden that will not be known. What you've said in the dark will be heard in broad daylight. What you have whispered to someone in the inner rooms will be shouted from the rooftops.

"My friends, don't be afraid of those who kill the body. Because that's *all* they can do. But I will show you who you need to fear. Fear the one who, after killing your body, has the power to throw you into hell. But fear *only* him.

"And always remember this: Five sparrows are sold for two pennies. And yet not one of them is forgotten by God. Indeed, the very hairs of your head are numbered. So don't be afraid. You are worth more than all the sparrows in the world."

Before us, the expectant listeners were now seated in orderly rows, with plenty of room for people to move about. Lazarus signalled that they were almost ready. I moved to finish up my teaching with the disciples.

"I tell you, whoever acknowledges me before men, the Son of God will also acknowledge before the angels of God. But he who disowns me before men will be disowned before those very same angels. And everyone who speaks a word against the Son of Man will be forgiven. But anyone who blasphemes against the Holy Spirit will not be forgiven.

"So in the days to come when you are brought before synagogues, rulers, and authorities—and you will be—don't worry about how you will defend yourselves or what you'll say. The Holy Spirit will teach you exactly what to say at exactly the right time. Okay?"

Then I turned to the assembled multitude and began. As was my custom, I began with a series of questions for my listeners, then invited questions from the audience. After a few minutes, a middle-aged man bolted to his feet and blurted out, "Teacher, tell my brother to divide the inheritance with me!" Then he sat down, blushing mightily.

Big James nudged his brother John: "*This'll* be interesting!"

"Man," I said, hoping the annoyance didn't show in my voice, "who appointed me arbiter between you? But I will say this to all of you: Watch out! Be on your guard against all kinds of greed. For a man's worth is not tied to the value or number of his possessions.

"Think about it this way: A certain rich man's land always produced a good crop each year until one year it produced a bumper crop. As he gazed over his fields he thought, 'What shall I do? I don't have the storage space for all this grain.'

"He thought about it a while and finally came up with a plan. 'Here's what I'll do,' he thought. 'I'll tear down my barns and build bigger ones. And once they're complete, I'll have plenty of room to store all of my grain and my possessions. And, at that point, I'll be able to say to myself, "Now you have plenty of good things laid up for the future. With this nest egg, it's time to take life easy—eat, drink, and be merry!"'

"But God had other plans for this rich man. He said, 'You fool! This very night your life will be threatened—and lost! Then who will get what you have stored away for yourself?'

"This is how it will be with *anyone* who stores up things for himself—but is not rich toward God."

I noticed that the twelve were nodding in a self-satisfied and smug manner, as if to say, "Thank God *we're* not like that." So, instead of addressing the crowd at large—as was my custom—I continued...but now looking directly at *them*!

"So here's my advice: Don't worry about your life, about what you will eat, or what you will wear. Life is much more than food and the body more than clothing. Consider the ravens: They don't sow or reap, they have no storerooms or barns, yet God feeds them. And how much more valuable are you than these birds? Besides, who can add a single hour to his lifespan by worrying? And since you can't do this little thing, why do you worry about the rest?"

Now the self-righteous smiles were gone.

"Or consider the lilies. They do not work or spin. And yet I tell you that Solomon in all his majestic splendor was not dressed as beautifully as a single lily. And if that is how God clothes a mere flower, which lives just a few days then wilts away, how much more will our Father in heaven clothe you—oh you of little faith?"

I'd finally struck a nerve.

"Likewise, do not set your heart on what you will eat or drink—just don't worry about it. For the pagan world lusts after and worries about things like that and your Father knows you need them. But it is more important that you seek his kingdom and these things will be given to you as well.

"In short, my friends, do not be afraid. Your Father is happy to give you the kingdom. Sell your possessions and give the money to the poor. Provide purses for yourselves that will not wear out. In other words, strive for a treasure in heaven—the kind of treasure that will not be exhausted, the kind of treasure no thief can ever touch, the kind of treasure no moth can ever destroy. For where your treasure is, your heart is as well."

Someone said from the fringes of the crowd, "The way you're talking, it's almost as if the end is near."

"Exactly!" I exclaimed, much to the surprise of the twelve. "Be dressed and ready for service and keep your lamps burning like servants waiting for their master to return from a wedding banquet. In this way, when he returns and knocks, they can immediately open the door for him—no matter if it is the second or third watch of the night. It will be good for those servants whose master finds them watching for his arrival. I tell you the truth, that happy master will then dress himself up in servants' garments, have the servants recline at the dining table, and *he* will wait on *them!*

"But, on the other hand, understand this: if the owner of the house had known when a thief was coming, he would not have allowed his house to be broken into. So you must be ready, because the Son of Man will come at an hour when you least expect it."

Peter shyly raised a hand to speak. "Uh, Master, sorry about this. But are you telling this parable just to us—or to everyone here?"

"Think of it this way, Peter: Imagine a faithful and wise manager. His master puts him in charge of his servants when he is away. When the master returns and finds the manager carefully doing exactly what he was told to do, the master will not only be very pleased, he'll probably put this manager in charge of all of his possessions as well.

"But suppose, just suppose, that this same manager thinks to himself, 'You know, my master won't be home for a long, long time.' So, with no one there to supervise him, he starts beating the servants, eating the master's food, and drinking his best wine.

"That manager is going to be surprised when the master returns home unexpectedly and finds him drunk! He's going to cut the manager into little pieces and toss him into the place where all unbelievers go.

"The servant who *knows* his master's will and does not get ready or does not do what he's supposed to do will receive a vigorous beating. But the servant who does not know his master's will and does something that deserves punishment will receive far fewer blows.

"This is the point: for everyone who has been given much, much will be expected. For everyone who has been entrusted much, much more will be asked."

"Yup," Nathanael said dourly, "he was talking to us."

But Peter didn't answer. He only shivered slightly in the bitter wind and drew his cloak tighter about his neck.

Still, I wasn't quite through with the twelve just yet.

"I have come to bring fire on the earth—and how I wish it were already kindled! But first, I have another baptism to endure. You can't imagine how distressed I will be until it is completed.

"In the meantime, did you really think I came to bring peace on earth? No! Instead, I've come bringing division. From now on, family members will be pitted against each other. Father will oppose son and son will oppose his father. Mothers will oppose their daughters and daughters will stand against their mothers. Mother-in-law against daughter-in-law, daughter-in-law against mother-in-law."

It was so quiet I could hear my own heart beating. The twelve and the multitude behind them sat silently, weighing what I'd said. To be honest, I'd surprised myself with the vehemence of my words.

HEALING ON THE SABBATH

The following day, we made the long journey back to Bethany. We arrived home the night before the Sabbath. At Mary and Martha's urging, I accepted an invitation to teach in one of the local synagogues in Bethany the following day. We'd carefully avoided synagogues in recent months, but it was hard to deny Mary and—especially—Martha when they asked for something. Martha was a most imposing person!

The teaching went well and the people of Bethany seemed very receptive. But as I was wrapping it up, a woman hobbled in. She was bent nearly completely double and obviously was in profound pain.

Lazarus leaned over and whispered, "She's been that way for the past eighteen years, Jesus. A spirit entered her one day and she's never been able to stand straight since."

The woman's misery struck me like a slap. I called to her and she bravely shuffled over to me. I couldn't stand to see her suffer another minute.

I placed my hands on her and said, "Woman, you are set free from your infirmity."

Immediately, she stood up, straight as a pine tree. The mask of pain disappeared from her face and she spontaneously began giving thanks to God.

Just then, the synagogue ruler came storming down from his seat of honor, frantically waving his hands the whole way.

"No, no, *no!*" he said indignantly. "There are six days for work. Do your healing on one of those days—not on the Sabbath!"

He was fat and perfumed and perspiring and he waddled after the healed woman, apparently to drag her out of his precious synagogue.

I stepped between them.

"You hypocrites!" I thundered. "Every Sabbath, each of you unties your ox or donkey from the stall and leads it to water. Then why can't this woman—this daughter of Abraham who has been bound by Satan for eighteen miserable years—be set free on the Sabbath from what has bound *her?!*"

The fat ruler's fleshy lips opened and shut several times like a fish out of water as he tried to think of something to say. The healed woman kept rejoicing and dancing. Two Pharisees left in a huff. Everybody else cheered and whistled and joined the woman in a praise song.

Peter bounded down amid the happy confusion, singing and dancing himself, and said, "Lord, is this what heaven will be like?"

"What shall I compare heaven to?" I pondered aloud. Finally, I answered. "Peter, the kingdom of heaven is like the yeast that a baker takes and mixes into a large amount of flour until it is worked throughout all of the dough. That's what the kingdom of heaven is like."

Peter stood still amid the swirling chaos.

"I was afraid you'd say something like that," he said, then resumed his singing and dancing.

That night, back at Mary and Martha's, in front of a fire, we discussed the immediate future.

"I hate to leave Bethany again," Nathanael said. "It's relatively safe here, the people are mostly receptive to what we preach, and the food's great!"

Martha giggled and ladled him out another bowl of stew.

Uh oh—something's happening here! I mused happily.

"So, Lord, what would *you* like to do?" John asked.

"While we are so close to Jerusalem, I'd like to slip in for the Feast of Dedication," I said. "After that, I'm with Nathanael— the fields are ripe in Perea."

"Jesus, *please* promise me that there will be no more scenes in the Temple Colonnade," Simon the Zealot implored.

The others laughed.

I smiled, but he knew my answer before I said it: "I'll do my best, Simon, but I can't promise anything. I have to be about—"

"I know, I know," Peter interjected, "...my father's business!"

But late that night, after all had gone to bed, I sat by the window, staring out into the night, with only the banshee wail of the wind to accompany me.

Oh Father, I'm so alone. Even among friends, I'm so alone. Sometimes, I don't think even these twelve understand half of what I'm trying to say.

But only the cold north wind answered that night.

THE NARROW GATE

We finally left Bethany after a long good-bye and we lingered on the short walk to Jerusalem, speaking at some of the tiny settlements and farms along the way. A few hardy souls followed us in the cold drizzle, some also heading for the Feast of Dedication.

I figured enough time had passed that we could again risk the more conventional entrance into Jerusalem, through the Golden Gate on the east wall, entering through Solomon's Porch. As we passed the tombs that dot the northern reaches of the Kidron Valley, a young farm boy caught up with me and asked, "Lord, are only a few people going to be saved?"

He's so young to be concerned about such things, I thought. *But life is difficult in these hard-scrabble farms. Look at him: his cheeks are pinched and hollow and his cloak barely covers his bony legs. Father, have mercy on him.*

"My young friend, make every effort to enter through the narrow door, because I tell you that many, many will try to enter it and fail," I said gently.

"Once the owner of the house gets up and closes the door, you will stand outside knocking and pleading for entrance, saying, 'Sir, I beg you, open the door for us.'

"But the owner will be forced to answer, 'I don't know you. I don't know who you are nor where you're from.'

"And you will answer, 'But we ate and drank with you and you taught in our streets.'

"But the owner will reply, 'I said before I don't know you or where you come from! Now leave this house, you troublemakers—before I call the guards!'

"And there will be weeping and wailing when you see Abraham, Isaac, and Jacob and all the prophets in the kingdom of God, but you yourselves will be thrown out.

"People will come from the east, west, north, and south and will take their places at the feast in the kingdom of God. And the last shall be first and the first shall be last."

The skinny young man nodded, then bowed slightly. "Thank you, good Teacher. It is an answer I will cherish—and live by."

ANOTHER ANGRY CROWD

But mere minutes after we finally entered the Temple, Makir—Blue Robe—came walking casually up. He hooked an arm around me and, for all the world, it looked like we were a couple of old friends chatting. But it was only a facade—Makir was badly frightened.

"Jesus, please, leave this place and go somewhere else! Herod wants to kill you!"

"Makir, go tell that fox this: 'I will drive out demons and heal people today and tomorrow, and on the third day, I will reach my goal.' In any case, I must keep going today and tomorrow and the next day—for, surely, no prophet can die outside of Jerusalem!"

I smiled, but I'm afraid Makir was too scared to see that I was teasing him.

"No, no, you must go," he begged. "The whole city is ready to turn on you."

That much was certainly true. It was an unusually fickle town.

"O Jerusalem, Jerusalem!" I lamented. "You kill the prophets and stone those sent to you. How often have I longed to gather your children together, as a hen gathers her chicks under her wings—but you were not willing. And now look! Your house is left to you vacant and destroyed. I tell you the truth, you will not see me again until you say, 'Blessed is he who comes in the name of the Lord.' "

Poor, confused Makir left, shaking his head. He wanted so badly to believe, and yet he was still chained by a lifetime of Pharisaic teaching!

Others in the small crowd heard our brief exchange and began peppering me with questions. Finally, one man said, "How long will you keep us in suspense? If you are really the Christ, tell us plainly, once and for all!" The others nodded vigorously. "Tell us! Tell us!"

Nathanael groaned, "Oh brother, here we go again!"

"I *did* tell you, but you do not believe," I said to my inquisitors. "The miracles I do in my Father's name speak for me. It doesn't matter, though, you don't believe because you're not my sheep. My sheep listen to my voice. I know them and they follow me. I give them eternal life and none of them will die. Moreover, no one can snatch them out of my hands. You see, my Father—who original- ly gave them to me—is greater than all. There is no power strong enough to steal them out of *his* hands. My Father and I are one."

The man who asked the question blanched, then began scream- ing incoherently, pointing at me. Others followed, howling, "Stone him! Stone him!"

In a flash, Simon and Judas were in front of me, sword and dagger drawn. But even as the Jews in the mob began picking up stones, I pushed between the two disciples and confronted those who were demanding my death.

"I have shown you many great miracles from the Father," I said calmly. "Before you kill me, please tell me which one it is you're about to stone me for."

"You fool!" the first man hissed through foam-flecked lips. "We are not stoning you for any miracle, but for basest blasphemy, pure and simple. You, a man—have just claimed to be God! Your own lips condemn you!"

"Ahh," I said, a slight smile forcing itself on my face, "then you have not read the Law. Don't you remember the passage that says, 'I have said you are gods'? If he called them 'gods'—that is, those people to whom the Word of God was given and the Scripture cannot be broken—what about the one whom the Father has set apart as his very own and sent into this world? Why then do you accuse me of blasphemy? Because I said, 'I am God's son?'

"Do not believe me unless I do what my Father does. But if I do it, even though you do not believe me, then believe the miracles that you may learn and understand that the Father is in me—and I am in the Father."

Alas, that broke the spell! The man dropped his stones and hurled himself at me, clawing and biting. Others around him launched themselves at us as well—although some immediately felt the power in Peter's knotted fists. Others in the back of the crowd began throwing stones, but most hit those who attacked us. Within seconds, bodies lay everywhere, bleeding and bruised. In the confusion, Simon led us to safety, moments before the Temple guards came running into the melee, clubs and truncheons flailing.

We took the alleys and back roads until we ended up at one of the few remaining safe houses in Jerusalem.

Then, under cover of darkness, we slipped out of town again, heading north toward Bethabara, where I'd first heard John the Baptizer preach, to the welcoming home of Zaccur.

It was nearly dawn when we arrived, exhausted and battered. John had some nasty deep bruises where he'd tried to shield me with his body from the stones. Peter had broken a knuckle on some hardheaded skull. We were cold, hungry, and lightheaded from lack of sleep.

The intensity of the naked hatred and violence in Jerusalem had stunned us all. It was a low moment in our ministry.

I will never see Jerusalem again—until my hour is come, I thought sadly.

As we staggered into Zaccur's house, a messenger from Bethany was waiting. He too was tired, covered with road dust, and red-eyed from lack of sleep.

"Jesus, Master," he gasped, "I was told I might find you here. It is Lazarus, the one you love. He's dying."

CHAPTER SIX

Contending with Blindness

THE RAISING OF LAZARUS

There was nothing else we could do that night. We collapsed in our makeshift beds.

I got up before the rest of my exhausted disciples for my morning prayers. A curious peace about Lazarus filled me.

Later that morning, as Nathanael and the others rose, they began pressing me to return to Bethany.

"We don't have much time," the messenger pleaded.

"Be at peace," I told them. "This sickness will not end in death. No, instead it is for God's glory so that the Son of Man may be glorified through it. Trust me."

Shaking his head, the messenger returned to Bethany.

Still, I know it must have mystified the twelve that I chose to remain in Bethabara two more days, occasionally teaching and healing, but mostly allowing them to gather their strength for the trials ahead.

At last I told them it was time to return to Judea.

Judas sprang to his feet. His face still purple from an errant stone, Judas had become increasingly sullen and brooding in recent months.

"Rabbi, are you mad?" he said. "Have you forgotten how the Jews nearly killed us all just days ago? And you want us to risk our lives—and yours—to return again? Do you have a death wish?"

I could see the torment on his face. *You honestly believe I may be mad, don't you, Judas?* I thought. *Or worse than a madman, you fear I may be a naive fool. A naive fool with miraculous powers perhaps, but a fool nonetheless.*

"Oh, Judas," I said as lovingly as I knew how, "aren't there twelve hours of daylight? And a man who walks in the daylight won't stumble. It is only when he walks at night, when there is no light, that he will stumble."

"Well, then, what about Lazarus?" Nathanael asked.

"Our friend Lazarus has fallen asleep," I answered, "but I am going there to wake him."

"Uh, if he sleeps, he'll get better," Nathanael said. "Won't he?"

"No, Nathanael, Lazarus is dead."

Eyes widened and jaws dropped.

"And for your sakes," I continued, "I am glad that I was not there so that you may believe. Even so, it's now time to go to him."

The twelve stared at each other, unspeaking, until Thomas broke the silence: "Let's go, too—so that we may die with him."

If it was a joke, it fell flat among the remaining disciples.

The day broke clear and cold, a wan sun barely strong enough to cast a decent shadow. There were few people about the cobbled Roman road south and we made good time.

When we reached Bethany, there were people everywhere. The small village was positively choked with visitors—and all heading for Mary and Martha's house.

"What's going on? What's happening?" Big James asked some of the people streaming past us.

"It's Lazarus," a woman answered. "He's dead. Been dead for four days. We've come from Jerusalem to comfort Mary and Martha. So have a lot of other people, it appears."

As we inched our way toward their familiar house, we suddenly encountered the formidable Martha standing squarely in the roadway. Nathanael began to run forward to greet her, but John wisely held him back. Mary was nowhere to be seen.

"Jesus!" she shouted. "If you had been here, my brother would not have died."

I said nothing. Giant tears spilled down her rosy cheeks.

At last, she stepped forward to embrace me. "Still, I know that—even *now*—God will give you *whatever* you will ask."

I smiled inwardly at the brave, fierce hope in her voice.

I brushed her tears away.

"Your brother will rise again."

"I know he will rise again in the resurrection on the last day," she stammered, her voice thick with emotion.

This time I took her hands and made her look straight at me.

"Martha, I *am* the resurrection and the life. Those who believe in me will live, even though they may someday die. And whoever believes in me will *never* die."

Long pause.

"Martha, do you believe this?"

She freed her hands, wiped her face, and said in a voice loud enough for all of the onlookers present to hear: "I believe! I believe that you are the Christ, the Son of God—who was to come into the world!"

Then she whirled and proudly marched back home.

Before we could follow, we were inundated by cold, hungry, hurting people.

A few minutes later, Mary rushed up, trailed by an entourage of weeping friends and wailing professional mourners. Martha followed their wake.

She threw herself at my feet. "Oh Master—if you had been here, Lazarus never would have died." Her thin body shuddered in great heaving sobs.

It broke my heart to see them like this.

I looked at Mary and asked, "Where have you lain him?"

"Follow me, Lord," she said clearly and loudly.

As we walked to the tomb, the depth of their loss overcame me as well. They had spent the past four days believing that their beloved brother was dead.

Around me, I vaguely heard the comments of the trailing crowd.

"See how much he loved Lazarus!"

"Why wasn't he here sooner?"

"He healed blind men—why couldn't he have kept Lazarus from dying?"

After a short walk, we reached the sprawling cemetery grounds, cold and barren, swept clean by the bone-chilling north wind. Lazarus's tomb, like so many others, was sealed by a small boulder.

I stood before the tomb and breathed a silent prayer. *Father, please heal this beloved brother. Please allow the life-force to reenter his earthly body. Please raise him from the sleep of death.*

"Take away the stone," I told those in attendance.

Several men stepped forward to begin rolling away the boulder, but Martha stopped them.

"Lord, he's been in there four days," she said. "The odor of death and decay will be unbearable. And I…I'm not sure I want to see him this way."

I smiled at her. "Did I not tell you that if you believed, you would see the glory of God today?"

Martha hesitated a moment, then nodded.

"Remove the stone," she told the men in her usual brisk manner. "Now."

Mary collapsed in another round of tears.

When the stone had been removed, I prayed aloud. "Father, I thank you that you have heard me. I always knew that you heard

me, but I say this for the benefit of the people standing here—
that they may believe that you sent me."

Now the only sound was the weird wailing of the wind as it
whistled among the cemetery grounds.

"Lazarus!" I shouted. "Come forth!"

Long seconds passed.

Then, staggering and shuffling because he was so tightly bound
by the bandages, Lazarus burst from the dark cave. He clawed at
his face bandages and shielded his eyes from the thin winter sun.

"He's alive!" came the shout from all directions.

Then Mary and Martha rushed to him and began tearing off
the remaining bandages, even as they showered him with kisses
and tears.

Then all of those in attendance, in one accord, stampeded forward to embrace us all, sing praises, and spontaneously dance
with joy.

Well, perhaps not *all* of those in attendance. Ever-vigilant
Simon the Zealot noticed a few slink off and head back for
Jerusalem.

"Tell Jesus I'll be back," he whispered to Little James, as he dug
in his ever-present bag for a suitable disguise. With that, Simon
was gone.

A Hard Teaching

We then headed due east for Archelais. We'd left word for
Simon to report back to us at a certain inn on the outskirts of Archelais, but he wasn't expected for
several more days. Fortunately, the weather broke for a few days
and it was relatively mild for early February. As a result, the
crowds following us swelled. While still in the mountainous
wastelands, I found an outcropping of rocks near a deep wadi,

climbed to the top, and spent several hours teaching to those who wanted to listen.

DINNER WITH TAX COLLECTORS

As always, Matthew had sent runners ahead of us to secure our food and lodging in Archelais, so our arrival wasn't unexpected. However, the appearance of some of his friends—tax collectors all—was a surprise. In fact, there was a large delegation waiting for us as we walked out of the scrubby hills into the plain around the city. Matthew had also arranged a meal for us.

And in their midst were our friends the Pharisees and teachers of the Law, though none of our old "favorites" were in sight. Though I never missed Goat-beard and Bald Pharisee, I would have rather had them standing before me than back in Jerusalem, plotting my death.

As we settled in to eat, one Pharisee said in a stage whisper to another, "Look at this rabble! This Nazarene welcomes sinners and eats with them!"

All eyes turned expectantly to me for a response.

"Here are three parables, for rabble and 'non-rabble' alike," I said.

First, I repeated the story of the shepherd with a hundred sheep, who leaves them to search for a single lost sheep.

"Now, suppose a woman has ten silver coins, but somehow loses one," I continued. "You know she's going to light a lamp, sweep the house, and search carefully until she finds it. And when she does find it, she's going to call her friends and neighbors and say, 'Rejoice with me! I have found my lost coin!'

"Friends, in the same way, I'm telling you there is rejoicing in heaven among the angels when one sinner repents."

A general murmur of agreement rippled through the crowd—save for the Pharisees who fumed silently.

They're not going to like this example, though, I thought.

"One last story: there was a man with two sons. The younger said to his father, 'Give me my share of the estate—now.' So the father reluctantly did so.

"The younger son soon took off for a big city in a distant land. In short order, he wasted everything he had on wild, riotous living. Unfortunately, the country was gripped in a severe famine. Work was scarce, food was even more so. In desperation, the younger son finally hired on as a worker, feeding pigs—the unclean animals par excellence. In time, he saw that even what the pigs were eating was better than what he had to eat.

"One day, sitting amid the pigs, he cried aloud, 'Even my father's hired men have food to spare—and here I am, starving slowly to death! I vow to return to my father and implore him, 'Father, I have sinned against heaven and against you. I am no longer worthy to be called your son. Please, have mercy on me and make me one of your hired hands!' And off for home he went.

"But while he was still a ways off, his father saw him coming and was filled with compassion. He ran to his younger son, threw his arms around him, and covered him with kisses.

"The son repeated what he'd carefully rehearsed to his father. But the father roared at his servants, 'Quick! Bring my best robe and sandals for my son. Bring a beautiful ring and put it on his finger. And bring a fat calf and kill it. Let's feast and celebrate tonight! My missing son has returned—he who was feared dead is alive!'

"And that's what they did.

"But when the hardworking older son heard the music and smelled the food, he came in from the fields. He grabbed a servant rushing by with a plate of food and asked him what was going on. The servant replied, 'Your brother has returned! Your father has killed the fattest calf and is celebrating his safe return!'

"Enraged, the exhausted older brother slumped by the front door and resisted all entreaties to enter. At last, his father went outside and pleaded with him to come inside to the party.

"But the older brother said, 'Look, I've slaved for you for years. I never disobeyed you, never gave you any trouble. Yet, in all that time, you never even gave me so much as a goat when I wanted to party with my friends. But when your youngest son returns, having squandered your property on prostitutes, you kill the fatted calf for him!' With tears in his eyes the older son said, 'How could you?'

"And the father said, 'My son, you are always with me and everything I have is yours. But we have to celebrate and be happy because your brother who was dead is alive again. He was lost—and now he's found!'"

As I expected, several arguments broke out—even among the sets of brothers in the disciples. It seems that none of the older brothers liked *that* particular parable!

DEBATE WITH PHARISEES

I concluded the teaching for that day as the winds began to pick up, and we headed for the appointed inn on the edge of Archelais. It was warmly furnished and a comfortable refuge from the elements.

Judas sullenly paid the innkeeper, then disappeared. In recent weeks, Judas had refused to talk to me. He spent most of his time alone, flipping his dagger into the sand or nearby posts. His spirit was in turmoil and some nights he would sneak away and not return until dawn.

After resting and making inquiries about Simon, the remaining ten disciples joined me on a short walk through town. I found a protected enclave, out of the wind, and sat down to teach the disciples. But before I could get started, a handful of Pharisees all-too-casually walked up. It didn't matter—having them there wasn't going to change what I was going to teach.

Meanwhile, the Pharisees, many of whom—judging by their exquisite clothes and jewels—loved their money dearly, sneered at me and mocked my words so loudly they made it hard for others to hear.

"*You* are the ones who justify yourselves before men!" I shouted over their din, "but God knows your hearts. What is highly valued among men is detestable in God's eyes."

"We are the keepers of the Law—not you!" one shouted back, as if that ended the discussion. "We're the ones doing God's will—not you!"

"The Law and the Prophets were proclaimed until John," I said evenly. "Since that time, the good news of the kingdom of God has been preached—and everyone is forcing his way into it. It is easier for heaven and earth to disappear than for the least stroke of a pen to drop out of the Law.

"The Law says, 'Do not commit adultery.' But I tell you that anyone who looks at a woman lustfully has already committed adultery with her in his heart.

"You teach, 'Anyone who divorces his wife must give her a certificate of divorce.' But I tell you that anyone who divorces his wife causes her to become an adulteress and anyone who marries the divorced woman commits adultery."

"How can you say that?" the Pharisees sputtered. "We're trying to build a fence around the Law and here you're..."

"What *am* I doing, Pharisee?" I asked as mildly as possible. "You say, 'An eye for an eye,' and 'a tooth for a tooth.' But I say, do not resist an evil person. If someone strikes you on the right cheek, turn to him the other also. If someone wants to sue you and take your tunic, let him have your cloak as well. If someone forces you to go one mile carrying his pack, go with him two miles. Give to the one who asks you, and do not turn away from the one who wants to borrow from you."

"But...but where is your authority to say this? Who are you quoting?" the Pharisees continued to interject, suddenly unsure of their ground.

"I'm not through," I said, now walking toward them. "You've said, 'Love your neighbor and hate your enemies.' But I say, *love* your enemies and *pray* for those who persecute you that you may be one of your Father's sons in heaven.

"You see, the Father causes the sun to rise on the evildoer as well as the good person and sends rain on the just and unjust alike. If you only love those who love you, what reward will you get? Even the tax collectors and these so-called 'sinners' here that you despise so much do that! And if you greet only your brothers, so what? Even the pagans do that! Be perfect, therefore, even as your heavenly Father is perfect."

The Pharisees were now backing wildly away from me, tripping over stones and fences, then scrambling back up—never taking their eyes from me. A couple finally wheeled and took off in a dead run, leaving only the youngest Pharisee behind.

"No! You've got it all wrong," he stammered. "No one can be perfect—I mean, we're trying to do the right things—that is, the Law says..."

I was afraid he was going to hurt himself, so I grabbed his tunic before he fell over a cord of wood.

"And what about those 'right things'?" I said, my voice softer now. "Be careful *not* to do those right things before men, Pharisee, to be seen by other men. If you do, you'll get no reward from your Father in heaven. Rather, when you do give to the needy, do not announce it with trumpets—as the *hypocrites* do in the synagogues and street corners so that you'll be honored by other men. No, I'm telling you, they received their reward then and there.

"But when *you* give to the needy, do not let your left hand know what your right hand is doing. Do it in secret! Then your Father, who sees what is done in secret, will reward you."

The young Pharisee sat heavily on the stack of wood and I released him. I stood between him and the rest of the crowd so that they couldn't see the tears in his eyes. When he had wiped his face, I sat next to him and looked out at those in attendance.

"Let me tell you a story," I told the crowd. "It is the story of two men. One was exceedingly wealthy. He dressed in purple and the finest linen and lived a life of luxury all his days. Outside the rich man's gate lay a beggar named Lazarus, covered in hideous sores, starving and pain-wracked, too weak to even keep the dogs from licking his wounds. Lazarus longed to eat even the crumbs from the rich man's table.

"One day, Lazarus died and the angels carried him to heaven to sit by Father Abraham's side. Coincidentally, the rich man died about the same time. But the rich man went to hell where he was tortured and tormented day and night.

"The rich man looked into heaven and saw Abraham, far, far away, with Lazarus sitting next to him. The rich man cried out, 'Father Abraham, have pity on me! Send Lazarus to dip the tip of his finger into water and cool my tongue—for I am in agony in this never-ending fire!'

"But Abraham replied, 'Son, on earth you enjoyed the good things of life, while Lazarus received nothing. And now he is being comforted here while you are dying by degrees in hell. But a great chasm exists between us so that those who want to go from here to you cannot, nor can anyone cross from hell to heaven to join us.'

"The rich man answered, 'Then, I beg of you, send Lazarus to my house for I have younger brothers still living there. Please, allow Lazarus to warn them, so that they too will not end up in this place of eternal torment.'

"But Abraham replied, 'They have Moses and the Prophets. Let your brothers listen to them.'

"The rich man wailed, 'Father Abraham, I know them. They will not listen. But if someone from the dead goes to them, they will repent.'

"Abraham sadly shook his head. 'If they do not listen to Moses and the Prophets, they will not be convinced even if someone rises from the dead.'"

I heard John and Peter whispering nearby.

"The master's telling a story within a story," Peter said.

"It's the Sign of Jonah business again," John answered back. "This is more than a parable—it is a prophecy."

"Agreed, my friend," Peter said, "but exactly what does it mean?"

Oh, my dear friends. I don't know how much more explicit I can be, I thought sadly. Then I warmly embraced the young Pharisee, who stumbled off, his mind obviously reeling with all that he'd just heard.

SIMON'S REPORT

It was growing late, so I took the disciples back to the inn. Once we returned, we were overjoyed to see Simon the Zealot. I worried about him whenever he undertook a dangerous mission, but he seemed to thrive on the danger.

As he warmed himself by the fire, he told all that he'd seen and heard since the raising of Lazarus from the dead in Bethany.

"I followed a group of Pharisees back to Jerusalem," Simon said tersely, "and they went straight to an emergency meeting of the Sanhedrin with the chief priests. All of our old 'friends' were present, along with Nicodemus. The Pharisees reported—fairly

accurately, I might add—what they had seen in Bethany and elsewhere."

By the fire's dancing light, I saw a raw, fresh scar on Simon's
forearm, but now was not the time to ask about it.

"Goat-beard spoke first," Simon continued. "He said, 'What
are we accomplishing? Here is a man who is performing many
miraculous signs. If we let him go on like this, everyone will
believe in him—and then the Romans will come and take away
our positions!'

" 'And our nation,' Nicodemus added blandly.

" 'Of course,' Goat-beard said impatiently.

"Then this year's high priest, a sinister, scheming fellow named
Caiaphas, spoke up. He turned to Goat-beard and his voice just
dripped with venom. He said, 'You know nothing! Nothing!
Don't you realize that it is better that one man die *for* the people
than let an entire people perish!'

"Goat-beard cowered in his presence and said nothing."

"I'd like to have seen that," Peter said bitterly.

Simon nodded. "Then, for the first time, he noticed that there
were several of us in the audience. So he ended the meeting, sent
us out, and continued meeting behind closed doors.

"What I found out later, nearly cost me dearly," Simon continued with a grimace.

Oh Simon! What have you done?

"But the gist of it is this: Caiaphas has apparently prophesied
that Jesus will...will *die* for the nation of Israel and the other scattered children of God."

"When, man, when?" We were all startled to hear Judas finally
speak up, a strange urgency in his words.

"Some...sometime this year," Simon said, eyeing his friend
closely.

"So what do you suggest?" Matthew asked.

"Stay out of Jerusalem, stay in the countryside," Simon said flatly, his words blurred by fatigue.

"Enough," I said. "Matthew, please bring Simon something to eat. I suspect he has not eaten in days."

"What's our next move?" Nathanael asked.

"What our next move always is," I said. "We pray."

"And then?" Nathanael persisted.

"North. To Galilee."

THE TEN LEPERS

Perhaps they were all too exhausted to argue with me. Perhaps they all believed me implicitly. Perhaps they knew that I needed to see my home, one last time. For whatever reason, when we left Archelais, the twelve trudged silently behind me.

The day broke raw and blustery, with ragged clouds racing across the sky. By midday, a light, cold drizzle was falling. By nightfall, it was a bitter, soaking rain. We paid exorbitant prices for a seedy inn inside the fortress of Alexandrium, nearly exhausting Judas's treasury bag. The following morning, still in a steady rain, we continued northward along the swollen Jordan River.

At last, as we neared the border between Samaria and Galilee, we passed a leper colony—actually, a scattered grouping of pitiful shacks and lean-tos. Since no one had followed us on this journey, Matthew himself had gone ahead to Nain to make arrangements for our meals and lodging. Somehow, word that we were coming filtered even to this starving, rotting band of lepers.

As we walked along the Roman road, a handful of lepers stood outside their huts and shouted, "Jesus! Master! Have pity on us!"

They looked like ragged scarecrows, living in filthy rags and bandages, stinking and stained. Most had mere clubs for hands and feet, and yet they leaned on one another in the driving rain, begging me for mercy—and healing.

Father, heal them, I prayed.

"Go!" I shouted back. "Show yourself to the priests."

Even from the road, we could see the color returning to their deathly white skin. They tore off bandages and showed each other whole, healthy fingers and toes. Then, as one, the ten dashed over the hill toward Nain to find a priest.

A few minutes later, a single former leper came racing back and threw himself at my feet. "Praise God! Thank you for my healing, Jesus of Nazareth! May God bless you for this wonderful miracle!"

From his accent, he was obviously a Samaritan.

I turned to John, "Weren't ten lepers cleansed? Where are the other nine? No one else returned to give thanks and praise to God—except this Samaritan."

I touched his head. "Rise and go—your faith has made you well."

REJECTED BY NAZARETH AGAIN

The journey from Nain to Nazareth is a short one. Even in the fog-shrouded mists of dead winter, the beauty of this rolling land struck me once again. I'd missed Galilee over the past year. Both Nazareth and Capernaum had turned against me, so this homecoming was bittersweet at best.

Always thinking ahead, Matthew had sent runners ahead to make quiet inquiries about our acceptance in both towns. As we crested the last hill before Nazareth, the runner from that city returned. He conferred briefly with Matthew, then both reluctantly approached me.

"It's no good, Jesus," Matthew said softly. Hepher has met in secret with our few remaining friends in Nazareth. They say there is great danger in Nazareth."

"And my family?" I asked him. "What of Mary my mother and my brothers and sisters?"

"It is a curious thing," Hepher replied, still gasping for breath. "There is talk that James, at least, has been heard to say that he now believes that you *are* the Christ. Another woman told me that Mary too is alleged to have admitted that privately. But the opposition is so stiff, that they rarely speak of you and instead keep mostly to themselves. But there was no way I could approach your family to confirm this without arousing suspicion—or making things harder on them."

"Thank you, Hepher, you have done well," I said.

I took one last long look at sleepy Nazareth, its edges softened by the gathering fog, then left.

Being Herded Toward Jerusalem

The twelve respected my need for privacy and we spoke little as we found the main east/west road from Sepphoris to Tiberias. It was in Tiberias, another seaport on the Sea of Galilee, that we would meet our other runner from Capernaum.

When we arrived in Tiberias the following day, the cold snap ended, the faint traces of frost on the ground disappearing in the morning sun. It was early March and the air was still cold—but not so cold as in Nazareth or Nain.

Our runner was waiting for us at the inn. His clothes were torn and his face was bruised and bloodied.

"My friend, what has happened?"

"Alas, Jesus, the Pharisees and lawyers have stirred up a hornet's nest in Capernaum," he wheezed, his ribs obviously sore and bandaged. "One of our former friends has sold out to the Herodians. They caught me trying to sneak into Maariah's house and roughed me up pretty good. If Maariah hadn't heard my cries for help and chased them away with her woodcutter's axe, I have no doubt that those thugs would have beat me to death. I'm only here because Peter's wife bribed some Roman soldiers to bring me to Tiberias."

"And my wife and mother-in-law, how are they faring?" Peter asked, his voice tinged with fear.

"Oh, no one dares to bother them," the runner said. "They are well respected in the community. But most of the other believers have gone underground."

"Do I need to go to them?" Peter asked.

"They told me to tell you to stay away, at least until tempers cool," the runner said, grimacing in pain.

That night, we had another visitor at the inn. It was Mary Magdalene and some of her friends. Magadala too had fallen sway to the poisonous threats of our enemies.

My adversaries were closing the net to the north.

"It is almost as if they're herding us southward, toward Jerusalem," Simon mused that night after prayers.

"We still have some strongholds in Perea, along the Jordan," Matthew suggested. "Perhaps we should head back south. What do you think, Jesus?"

My family, Peter's family, Mary's family in Magadala—how many others have already suffered for my sake? How many more will suffer before this string is played out?

"Uh, Jesus?" Matthew interrupted my thoughts with a polite cough. "Shall we go to Perea?"

"Yes," I said absently. "Perea is fine."

And after Perea, once more to Jerusalem.

For the last time.

TEACHING AT PEREA AND AMATHUS

Simon's uncanny instincts proved right once again. As we moved slowly in Perea, we found strong pockets of support throughout the countryside. Some hostile Pharisees and Herodians were present, to be sure, but they hadn't made much headway here. Most Pereans were simply too independent-minded. The Pharisees hadn't helped their cause by sending out some of their more extreme representatives. To the Pereans, who valued common sense above all, some of their interpretations of the Law appeared just plain silly. For instance, certain Pharisees would give food to a starving beggar on the Sabbath only if he stuck his hand inside a Pharisee's home—so that the Pharisee wouldn't have to reach outside. They also said women couldn't look into mirrors on the Sabbath—because they *might* see a grey hair and be tempted to pull it out!

At Amathus, we attracted our largest crowd since the raising of Lazarus in Bethany. After a spirited morning of teaching and arguing with the Pharisees about adultery, I stood around talking with the twelve.

A group of women suddenly appeared, their children—of all ages—in tow. They surged through the lawyers and disciples and begged me to touch them. I think the disciples were a little miffed at the interruption of the "serious" discussion, and quickly scolded the mothers for barging in—then shooed them away.

I reacted immediately. Some of these twelve have been traveling with me for nearly three years, and they *still* don't get it!

Few things raised my indignation—or anger—as quickly as a wrong done to innocent people or a willful blindness to human suffering. I dismissed disciple and Pharisee alike, then motioned the children to me.

As the adults watched incredulously, I addressed the lot of them: "Let the children come to me—and do not hinder them. For to such belongs the kingdom of heaven."

I could tell from their shocked looks that none of them thought that children were significant enough to bother with while they went about "God's business." These precious children were merely an annoyance to them.

"Truly, I say to you, whoever does not receive the kingdom of God like a child shall not enter it."

I hugged each child and blessed each one individually, while the disciples and Pharisees continued to stand around, cooling their heels and muttering among themselves.

These Pharisees don't have a chance. They are filled with their own importance. They believe that fanatical devotion to the nuances and thousand peculiarities of the Law are enough. They are the antithesis of a childlike acceptance.

And yet, one of our most ancient sayings states that the children of even godless pagans will be included in heaven.

It is something I shall need to reinforce with the twelve in the days left to us.

"Teacher."

I looked around and was startled to find a well-dressed man kneeling at my feet. I'd apparently been lost in thought.

"A thousand pardons, good Teacher. But may I ask you a question?"

"By all means."

"What must I do to be saved?"

"Why do you call me 'good'?" I asked him, as I helped him back to his feet. "No one is good—except God alone.

"Now, as to your question. I'm sure you know the commandments: 'Do not murder, do not commit adultery, do not steal, do not give false testimony, do not defraud, honor your father and mother.'"

"Of course, Teacher. All of these I have kept since my childhood."

I could tell he was completely sincere, completely earnest. I also sensed that he was an honorable young man. But I could also see that greed was leading him on the path toward a bleak future. I placed my hand on his shoulder.

"Then there's only one thing left for you to do: Go, sell everything you have and give it to the poor so that you'll have treasure in heaven. Then come and follow me."

The man looked at me for long seconds, his mind a'blur with conflicting thoughts and emotions. At last, his face fell and he turned slowly away and walked off, an impressive entourage of servants and slaves trailing behind him.

As he disappeared down the street, I said to my disciples, "How hard it is for the rich to enter the kingdom of heaven!"

Judas rushed up. "Think, man! Our treasury is all but empty. We could have used a rich, powerful friend like that! Why'd you drive him away so callously—are you mad?"

But the glint of madness was in Judas's eye—not mine.

"Children," I said wearily, "let me repeat—it is exceedingly hard to enter the kingdom of heaven. It is easier for a camel to go through the eye of a needle than for a rich man to enter the kingdom of heaven."

Judas turned and spat on the ground. "Then who *can* be saved?"

I tried to catch Judas's eye, but he wouldn't look up. "For men and women, this is impossible. But for God, all things are possible."

Peter stepped forward. "Master, we've left everything—everything!—to follow you. What... what can we expect?"

I smiled at Peter. "Peter, anyone who has left his home or brothers or sisters or mother or father or children or fields for me and the gospel will receive a hundred times as much in this present age as he or she will receive—along with the persecutions—in the age to come, the age of eternal life. But one word of warning: again, many who are first will be last and the last will be first."

"What is this kingdom of heaven you keep talking about?" one onlooker asked. "Who'll be there?"

"The kingdom of heaven is like a vintner who once went out early in the morning to hire some laborers for his vineyard," I said. I could see Matthew furiously scribbling notes as I talked. In recent weeks, he'd begun writing down all of my parables, then asking me about them later.

"After agreeing with the laborers for a denarius a day, he sent them to his vineyard. After a few hours, the vintner saw some other men standing idle in the marketplace, so he went to them and said, 'Why don't you go on out to my vineyard and I'll pay you a fair amount at the end of the day.' So they did. The vintner did this several more times during the day, finding unemployed men at different hours and offering them work in his vineyard.

"When the evening came, the vintner said to his steward, 'Call the laborers in and pay them their wages, beginning with those we hired last, right up to the ones we hired this morning.' And that's just what the steward did—and he paid every man a denarius each.

"Well, those who'd been there all day started muttering and grumbling among themselves—they thought they'd receive more. So the boldest of the workers walked up to the vintner and said, 'Some of these men only worked an hour or so, and yet you paid them the same amount you paid those of us who have been out working in the hot sun all day!'

"But the vintner replied to them, 'Friend, I'm not cheating you. You freely agreed to work for me for an entire day for a denarius—didn't you? Take what belongs to you and go. It's my choice to pay the last workers the same as I paid the first. It's my prerogative if I want to do that with my own money. Or do you resent my generosity?'

"Again I say to you, the last will be first, and the first will be last."

Judas again snorted in derision at the conclusion of this parable. "More gibberish! I can't believe I'm following this man to certain death in Jerusalem—and I'm subjecting myself to this mystical balderdash along the way for the privilege!"

But the others mulled it over carefully.

THE REQUEST OF THE MOTHER OF JAMES AND JOHN

After a few days, we left Amathus, crossed the Jabbok River, and took the road back toward Archelais. Since the weather was holding, I was tempted to cross the hills to Gedara, but I began to feel an urgency to reach Jerusalem.

As we walked in the cool, blustery weather, Thomas caught up with me. "I've been thinking about what Judas said. We're not *really* going to Jerusalem, are we? I mean, it doesn't make a lot of sense. Does it?"

I called the twelve together. "Not only are we going to Jerusalem, the Son of Man will be handed over to the chief priests and scribes and Gentiles—just as the prophets predicted. He will be mocked, spit upon, whipped and—eventually—killed. But on the third day, he will rise again. Do you understand?"

But they didn't.

BLIND BARTIMAEUS

When it came time to leave Jericho the next morning, a great crowd followed us out, cheering and calling my name.

Just outside the city walls sat a blind beggar. When he heard the ruckus and my name being shouted, he screamed, "Jesus! Son of David! Have mercy on me!"

Others told him to be quiet, but he persisted.

"Who is that?" I asked Zacchaeus.

"That is Bartimaeus, son of Timaeus," Zacchaeus said, "a sad case—blind since birth."

"Have mercy on me, Son of David!" Bartimaeus howled, but with renewed urgency.

"Zacchaeus, bring him to me," I said.

Zacchaeus waddled over and said, "Bartimaeus, be brave! Jesus is calling to you!"

Bartimaeus sprang up, tossed off his mantle, and took Zacchaeus's arm.

When they were standing in front of me, I said, "What do you want me to do for you?"

Bartimaeus said, "Lord, let me receive my sight."

"Let your eyes be opened," I said. "Now go your way—your faith has made you well."

Immediately, the cloudiness disappeared in Bartimaeus's eyes and he shouted, "Praise God! I can see! And praise Jesus, his son!"

Others took up the chant.

Bartimaeus grabbed my hand and kissed it and said, "Lord, where are you going?"

"I am going to Jerusalem," I said quietly.

"Lord, I will follow you to hell!" Bartimaeus said.

I looked to the east, toward Jerusalem.

"Dear Bartimaeus, I fear you will shortly get your chance."

And we left for Jerusalem.

For the last time.

CHAPTER SEVEN

Jerusalem Again—
The Last Days

AT BETHANY

But first, I wanted to stop in Bethany, to see Mary, Martha, and Lazarus again.

When we arrived—thanks no doubt to Matthew's meticulous planning—they had prepared a lovely dinner in my honor. It was a glorious meal surrounded by those I loved. The food was good; the talk was better.

But in the midst of the chaos, so quietly I almost didn't notice her at first, Mary slipped in. She gracefully knelt at my feet, opened an ampulla, and poured the contents on my feet. It was pure nard, an expensive perfume, and the lovely fragrance filled the house.

Then, weeping silently, she began to wipe my dusty feet with her hair.

I was so touched, I nearly cried myself.

Then, when I saw Martha, holding a giant mixing bowl, beaming at us—I *did* cry.

But the moment was just as quickly shattered. Judas jumped up, snatched the nearly empty treasury purse from his belt, and shook it at me. His handsome face was clouded with anger.

"Jesus! Why wasn't this perfume sold and the money given to the poor? It must be worth a year's wages! Meanwhile, we're always broke!"

For the first time, the usually jovial Nathanael stood menacingly.

"I seem to notice that no matter how little money we have, *you* always seem to eat well, Judas."

He took another step forward.

"In fact, now that I think about it, there always seemed to be plenty in the treasury when Matthew kept the purse."

John and Lazarus sprang up and separated the two. But Judas wasn't through yet.

"Answer me, Jesus. How can you lie there and let her waste that money while the poor starve outside our door?

"Leave her alone, Judas," I said.

I was tired. Tired of dealing with Judas. Tired of finessing the Pharisees. Tired of constantly traveling, constantly preaching, constantly placing those I loved in danger. I touched Mary's cascade of raven-black hair.

"Mary intended to save this perfume for the day of my burial. The poor will always be among us. But you will not always have me with you."

Judas barked a short, ugly laugh, then made a great show of stomping out the door. In the doorway, he almost collided with Simon the Zealot.

Simon?!

I hadn't even noticed that Simon wasn't among us.

Simon and Judas glared at each other, the hate so thick you could feel it like sea spray on the bow of a fishing boat. Then Judas was gone.

Simon rushed to my side and motioned to Lazarus.

"We've got problems, Rabbi," he said in his usual clipped manner. "The large crowd that's milling around outside your door has caught the attention of the chief priests. The word on the street is that they're now making plans to kill you as well, Lazarus. Your resurrection has caused quite a stir—and the priests don't like it."

I nodded, but Lazarus took the information in stride.

"Let 'em do their worst," he said. "It's hard to frighten someone who's already died once."

Even grim-faced Simon smiled. Then he turned to me.

"Jesus, I beg you. Call off this insane plan to return to Jerusalem tomorrow for the Passover Feast. The town's too volatile; there's no way I can guarantee our safety. The chief priests and Pharisees are just itching to murder someone."

"Thank you for all you've done—and will yet do, Simon called the Zealot," I said. "But this is something I *have* to do. Surely you—of all the twelve—understand that."

He stared evenly at me for long seconds, his eyes burning fiercely from a face crisscrossed with the scars of a thousand fights. Then he nodded as well.

"Then do what you have to do, Nazarene. I will be proud to be by your side."

Sometime during the night, Judas returned home.

TRIUMPHAL ENTRY INTO JERUSALEM

At dawn on Sunday, we headed for Jerusalem. I had hoped that by leaving early, we wouldn't be at the forefront of a column of people trooping into the Holy City but—alas—most were waiting expectantly for us to emerge from the home of Mary, Martha, and Lazarus. I wasn't sure what effect a crowd this size would have on the Roman garrison guarding the gates, nor was I sure I could slow the momentum even if I tried. Some young men, obviously messengers, bolted ahead of the crowd and disappeared up the road toward Jerusalem.

As we neared the Mount of Olives, I sent Thomas and Andrew north to the little village of Bethphage at the base of the mountain.

"Go into the village," I said, "and you will immediately find a colt tied to a post. Untie the colt and bring him to me."

Thomas's eyes were wide with wonder. "Uhhh, Lord, what if the owner says something along the lines of, 'That's *my* colt. That's not *your* colt. Why are you taking *my* colt?' "

"Tell him, 'The Lord has need of it.' "

Still shaking his head, Thomas trotted on ahead with Andrew.

A short while later, they reappeared, leading a frisky colt on a rope.

Thomas handed me the rope. "It happened just like you said it would," he said. "Sorry I doubted you."

He and Andrew threw their outer garments on the colt's back as we neared the Temple and the Golden Gate.

I stopped for a moment to speak only to the twelve:

"Oh, Jerusalem! I wish that even today you knew the elements of peace, not hate. But for now, they are hidden from your eyes. And, because of that, in the days to come, your enemies will surround you and hem you in on every side. Then they will utterly destroy you and leave not one stone standing—all because you did not know the moment of your visitation."

Already I could see people lining the road and standing by the gate, waving tree branches and palm fronds and cheering wildly. Soon those following us took up the cheers.

"Hosanna!"

"Blessed is he who comes in the name of the Lord!"

"Blessed is the kingdom of our father David that is coming!"

"Hosanna in the highest!"

I mounted the colt and rode toward the gate under the watchful eyes of the Roman guard. Some in the crowd threw their garments on the road before me.

It was a dizzying, heady spectacle and I watched the twelve closely. Save for Simon, they were caught up in the excitement of the moment, waving to the onlookers, looking for all the world like victorious gladiators in the arenas for an adoring public.

Suddenly, a knot of people separated themselves from the cheering crowd. It was Goat-beard and a handful of his favorite bullies and sycophants.

"Teacher," screamed Goat-beard over the roar of the crowd, "command your disciples to stop this heresy!"

"If these were silent," I said, "the very stones would cry out!"

Disgusted, Goat-beard stormed away.

HEALING AND TEACHING AT THE TEMPLE

Once inside the Temple grounds, Goat-beard and the Temple guards were able to quickly break up the demonstration—brutally and efficiently. As the crowds dispersed, we worked our way to the Court of Gentiles.

From every corner of the portico, the blind, the lame, the ill came streaming toward us, begging for healing. And I stayed, healing them all until late in the day.

At one point, in mid-afternoon, the newly healed, their families and children began singing, "Hosanna to the Son of David!" It was a spontaneous display of affection and I was deeply moved.

Of course, the priests and scribes had to spoil it. They came rushing out of their cubbyholes and schools and shouted at me, "Stop that! Stop that! Jesus—don't you hear what they are saying?"

I looked up from the child with the crooked spine I was praying over and said, "Yes, I hear. But have *you* never read,

'Out of the mouth of babes and the sucklings thou hast brought perfect praise'?"

They *hated* it when I quoted Scripture to them!

When the child stood up, her spine healed and straight, the priests and scribes drifted away.

By evening, I was exhausted—as tired as I can ever remember being in my life. But a large crowd still remained, clamoring to be heard, to be healed, to just be near someone who cared. Finally, we made to return to Bethany to spend the night. But as we were leaving the Court of Gentiles, a group of Greeks approached Philip, who introduced us.

They asked about following me.

"The hour has come for the Son of Man to be glorified," I said wearily. "Truly, unless a kernel of wheat falls to the ground and dies, it remains only a single seed. But if it dies, it produces many seeds. The man who loves his life will lose it, while the man who hates his life in this world will keep it forever. Whoever serves me must follow me—and where I am, my servants will be also. My Father will honor the ones who serve me."

"But...but this sounds like your hour is short," one of the Greeks protested.

"Yes, my heart is troubled," I admitted, "and what shall I say? 'Father, save me from this hour?' But, no. It was for this very rea-son—*this very hour*—that I came. Father—I glorify your name!"

Suddenly, it was like all the air was sucked out of the pavilion. All sound ceased. I felt weightless, suspended in space.

And that awfulwonderfulgloriousscarywarmingempowering voice thundered again from heaven: *I HAVE GLORIFIED IT AND WILL GLORIFY IT AGAIN.*

Then it was gone.

The crowd erupted in an instantaneous cheer. Some fell to the ground and praised God, others claimed it was only thunder—in a cloudless sky!

I turned back to the Greeks, now pale-faced and perspiring. "This voice was for your benefit, my friends—not mine. Now is the time for the judgment on this world. Now is the time that the prince of this world will be driven out. But when I am lifted up from the earth, I will draw *all* men to myself."

Some of those who heard what I said spoke up: "We have heard from the Law that the Christ will remain forever. So how can you say 'The Son of Man must be lifted up?' And just who *is* this Son of Man?"

These weren't angry, accusing questions like those of some Pharisees. No, these were honest, heartfelt questions from people who were genuinely confused.

"You are going to have the light just a little while longer," I told them. "Walk while you have the light—before the darkness overtakes you. The man who walks in the dark does not know where he is going. Put your trust in the light while you have it so that you may become sons of men."

Some stood listening with every fiber of their being. Some walked away in disgust. A few ran off, doubtless to find a Pharisee or priest.

Then we continued out of the Temple and home to Bethany.

Despite my fatigue, I slept only fitfully that night.

So much to do, so little time.

CLEANSING THE TEMPLE

I woke even earlier than usual Monday for my morning prayers and had to wake my tired and foot-sore disciples to join me for our return to Jerusalem. With much grumbling and groaning, all twelve eventually joined me on the road. It was much too early to wake Mary or Martha—who would insist on fixing us breakfast.

We were physically and emotionally spent, but the urgency I'd felt since returning to Galilee was only heightened. I was *compelled* to keep moving, to accomplish as much as possible in the time left to me.

En route, I saw a fig tree by the side of the road. We'd all missed breakfast and my stomach rumbled constantly. But when we approached it, I saw that it was barren.

I was tired, hungry, and perhaps still a little angry.

"May no one ever eat fruit from you again!" I snapped.

It was in that mood that we entered the Temple. Beneath its stately colonnades, the moneychangers and animal salesmen were already busy. Even as we watched, frightened, illiterate farmers were cowed and bullied into buying and selling certain animals or brazenly cheated in the exchange. As I stood watching, my anger rising, crowds of people streamed past us, trampling through the Temple grounds, en route from one gate to another.

I was still grieving from the day before over the harsh, ruthless treatment of my followers by the Temple guards.

Now I was saddened how—amid the street noise, the haggling of the vendors, the cries of the animals—the Gentile converts came to the Temple to try and pray and worship my Father.

I was tired of Goat-beard and his gang following me endlessly, pointing and whispering, standing just out of earshot, plotting my death.

And I was pained to see the ever-present rows of Roman soldiers clattering through the streets or staring down from the walls, ready to strike mercilessly at a moment's notice at any perceived disruption of the *Pax Romana*.

I can stand this no longer!

I grabbed a whip of cords made out of thongs from a startled cattle drover.

Then, with a shout that came from the depths of my soul, a shout that cut through the general confusion and cacophony of the marketplace, I waded into the stalls, overturning the tables of the moneychangers, knocking over the seats of those who sold pigeons, shattering cages and pens, scattering the vendors before me.

My stunned disciples stood motionless. None of the merchants made a move to stop me. Even the guards seemed paralyzed.

Those before me scattered like sheep, scrabbling on all fours to get out of my way.

"It is written, 'My house shall be called a house of prayer'— but you have made it a den of robbers!" I roared.

After long minutes, a group of Jews timidly approached me and asked, "By what sign are you doing this to us?"

And standing atop piles of money, at the center of a maelstrom of merchants chasing lost doves and bleating lambs, I paused and wiped my brow.

"Destroy this Temple and in three days I will raise it up," I said.

One of the men scoffed and said, "It has taken forty-six years to build this Temple—and you are going to raise it in three days?"

I handed the man the scourge and walked away, my numb disciples in tow.

One man in the crowd of onlookers muttered, "Isn't it said that when the true Messiah comes, he will cleanse and reform the Temple?"

Others around him nodded in agreement.

All except Simon the Zealot. "Jesus," Simon said, shaking his head, "you just sealed your death warrant. You just enraged the most powerful, most ruthless men in Jerusalem, men who are even

now plotting your death. This is something the ruling and priest-
ly classes cannot ignore."

I grabbed him around the neck in a sweaty bear hug.

"I know. Now let's get to work."

TEACHING AT THE TEMPLE AGAIN

Again, the needy and the hurting flocked to us, appearing—it
seemed—from thin air.

But before long, a procession of chief priests, elders, and
Pharisees paraded importantly toward us. They pushed their way
through the sick and began peppering me with questions. Most
had to do with who and what I claimed to be—and represented.

"When a man believes in me, he does not believe in me only,
but in the One who sent me," I said. "When he looks at me, he
sees the One who sent me. I have come into the world as a light
so that no one who believes in me should stay in darkness.

"As for the person who hears my words but does not keep
them, I do not judge him. For, as I have said before, I did not
come to judge the world, but to save it. There is another Judge for
the one who rejects me and does not accept my words. The very
words that I spoke will condemn him on the last day. For you see,
I do not speak of my own accord, but the Father who sent me
commanded me what to say and how to say it. I know that his
command leads to eternal life. So whatever I say is just what the
Father has told me to say."

One man, dressed in rich clothes, stood listening nearby, tears
streaming down his face. He reached a hand to me and I recognized him as a member of the Sanhedrin.

"I am Joseph, originally from Arimathea. I believe."

"Bless you, Joseph," I said.

The arguing and disputing consumed most of the rest of the
day, severely curtailing the amount of teaching and healing I was

able to do. Finally, shortly before dusk, we made the two-mile walk back to Bethany. Simon's sources said it was still not safe to remain in Jerusalem overnight.

A QUESTION OF AUTHORITY

On Tuesday morning, we trudged back into Jerusalem—but only after Martha and Mary insisted we leave with a proper breakfast. It wasn't long before we passed that same poor old fig tree. It was withered into a bare shadow of its former self.

Naturally, Peter *had* to point it out.

"Rabbi! Look! The fig tree you cursed yesterday has withered!"

"Truly, I tell you all, have faith in God and never doubt," I said. "If you do, even if you say to the Mount of Olives over there, 'Rise up and jump into the Great Sea'—it will happen! So whatever you ask in prayer, believe that you will receive it—*and you will!* And whenever you stand praying, first forgive anyone you have something against—so that your Father in heaven may forgive you as well."

This time when we entered the Golden Gate, a delegation of priests, scribes, Temple guards, and Pharisees—including our old buddy Bald Pharisee—were waiting on us. Bald Pharisee stood directly in my path, his arms folded, his feet firmly planted. As always, a crowd was gathering, expecting another show.

"Jesus of Nazareth!" he said theatrically, "by what authority have you done the things you've done here in recent days? Who gave you this authority?"

"A fair question," I answered. "Tell you what: you answer a question from me first. If you answer it, I will tell you by what authority I do what I do."

Bald Pharisee reluctantly nodded his assent—but didn't move.

"Here's my question," I said. "Was the baptism of John from heaven or from men?"

Bald Pharisee's massive, granite-like brow furrowed briefly. Then he ponderously turned and questioned the scribes and priests standing at his side. They argued furiously among themselves for several minutes, shooting glances my way all the while.

At one point, I heard Bald Pharisee say, "If we say, 'From heaven,' then he will say, 'Why didn't you believe him?'"

But a short, fat scribe said, "But if we say, 'From men'—then this crowd around us will explode, for everyone believes that John was a divine prophet!"

Finally, Bald Pharisee turned back to me. "We...uh...do not know." His bald pate and cheeks flushed scarlet.

The crowd exploded into cheers and laughter—all at Bald Pharisee's expense.

"Then neither will I tell you by what authority I do these things," I said with a pleasant smile—and we pushed past Bald Pharisee onto the Temple grounds, and then beyond.

We found a large open area outside the Temple walls, just under the pinnacle of the Temple, and I settled in to teach. Bald Pharisee and his gang followed, but kept their silence.

And it was at them that I addressed the following parables:

"Tell me what you think of this story," I said cheerfully. "A man had two sons. He went to the first and said, 'Son, go and work in the vineyard today.' But the son answered, 'I will not.' But afterward, he felt guilty and went to the vineyard.

"The father then went to the second son and asked him to go to the vineyard and work as well. The second son said, 'I'll go, sir.' But he never made it to the vineyard."

I looked directly at Bald Pharisee and said, "Which of the two did the will of his father?"

I could see that—despite himself—Bald Pharisee was intrigued. He thought a moment and said, "Why, the first son, of course."

"Truly, I say to you, the tax collectors and the prostitutes will enter the kingdom of heaven before you! For John the Baptizer came to you with the way to righteousness—and you did not believe him. But the tax collectors and prostitutes *did* believe. And even later, even after you *saw* the truth of John's words, you still will not repent and believe him."

Bald Pharisee's face contorted with rage and he balled his massive hands into fists. He wheeled to leave, but I stopped him with a word.

"Wait! I've got one more parable, one I think you need to hear—if you dare."

Bald Pharisee stood glowering at me, but he made no more moves to leave.

"This one is about a man who planted a vineyard," I said, never taking my eyes off Bald Pharisee. "He planted a hedge around it, built a winepress and a tower beside it, and rented it out to tenants. Then the owner left for another country.

"When the time came, the master sent a servant to the vineyard to tell the tenants to harvest the crop and pay his rent. But the tenants grabbed the servant, beat him, and sent him back to his master empty-handed. The master sent a second servant, but the tenants beat him even worse and he limped home empty-handed. A third servant returned grievously wounded.

"Finally, the master said, 'I'll send my beloved son. Surely these tenants will respect my son.' And so the master sent his son.

"But when the tenants saw the master's son arriving, they huddled together and said, 'This is the heir! Let's kill him and then we'll get his inheritance!' And that's what they did—they brutally murdered the master's son."

A gasped shock swept through the crowd—this was something they didn't expect. Bald Pharisee kept staring at me through slitted eyes, but he was listening.

"What will the owner of the vineyard do?" I continued. "You *know* what he'll do! He will return and kill the miserable wretches who murdered his son and give the vineyard to other tenants."

I stood and squarely faced Bald Pharisee and his compatriots.

"Have you never read the Scriptures? 'The very stone which the builders rejected has become the head of the corner. This was the Lord's doing and it is marvelous in his eyes. Everyone who falls on that stone will be broken to pieces—but when it falls on any one, it will crush him!'"

I heard one scribe say in faltering words to another—"He's talking about us!"

Even at a distance of several yards, I could see the veins popping on Bald Pharisee's forehead. He motioned for those with him to apprehend me.

But as the various scribes and Pharisees made the first menacing steps toward me, those in the crowd turned and formed a human wall between us. Some picked up stones. Bald Pharisee weighed the odds, found them wanting, and left.

Still, we thought it prudent to move to another part of the Holy City. We ventured southward away from the Temple, eventually arriving at the Pool of Siloam, near the southernmost gate, called the Ashpot or Tekoa Gate. Again, I settled in and began to teach. And again, a crowd quickly gathered. In their midst were a few Pharisees and Herodians—though none that I immediately recognized.

After a while, the Pharisees moved to the front and asked pleasantly, "Teacher, we know that you are true and teach the way of God, regardless of the cost. Perhaps you can answer this puzzling question for us. Is it lawful to pay taxes to Caesar or not? In other words, should we pay them or not?"

Their words oozed sincerity, but I could see their hearts.

"Why are you putting me to the test?" I asked. "Please bring me the money required for the tax."

Someone produced the necessary gold coin. I looked at it a moment and said to the Pharisees, "Whose likeness and inscription is found on this coin?"

The Pharisee holding the coin smirked and said, "Why, Caesar, of course."

"Good," I answered promptly. "Now render to Caesar the things that are Caesar's and render to God the things that are God's."

A hush fell over the crowd. For once, they didn't laugh at the Pharisees. The Pharisee nodded quickly, took his coin, and resumed his place at the back of the crowd.

After a short lunch break, we resumed our teaching in the same spot. The crowd was larger now and including, according to the ever-vigilant Simon, a number of Sadducees. I spoke until my voice began to rasp.

At last, it was time to return to Bethany. We decided to return via the Temple. We stopped for a breather outside of the treasury and watched the carnival of people proceeding around us. A steady stream of people passed the treasury, including a number of wealthy Jews who made a big deal of depositing large amounts of money in public—often to applause from onlookers.

But at one point, a poor, threadbare widow came, quietly produced two small copper coins, dropped them in, and slipped away.

I marveled at her faith and told my disciples, "This is the truth: I'm telling you that this poor widow has put in more than all those who are contributing to the treasury. For they all contributed out of their excess wealth. She alone, out of her poverty, deposited everything she had."

Then we continued onward. But by now, I was so fatigued I could barely put one sandal in front of another. We crept eastward toward Bethany at a snail's pace. Most of the disciples were equally exhausted.

With the sun's last rays, we rested in a copse of trees on the side of the Mount of Olives, still more than a mile from Bethany. The rest of the journey, alas, would have to be completed in darkness.

THE APOCALYPSE

While the others scattered, trying to find materials to craft torches in the fast-waning light, Peter, James, John, and Andrew sought me out as I sat alone.

"Jesus, all these things you've said over the past couple of days, the destruction of the Temple, the death and resurrection of the Son of Man—everything—what will be the sign of your coming and of the end of the age?"

As the others filtered back, busily weaving reeds, hay, twigs, and moss into makeshift torches, I shared with them what I knew of the final hours.

"Be careful that no one leads you astray," I said. "Many will come in my name, saying, 'I am he—the Christ!'—and they will mislead many.

"And then you will hear of wars and rumors of wars. But don't be afraid, for this must take place, although the end will not come right away.

"First, nations will rise against nations and kingdoms against kingdoms. Then there will be earthquakes and famines across the world. And this is only the beginning of the great suffering to come."

By now, all twelve had crowded around me, their crude torches whipping wildly in the brisk March winds. Despite their aching joints and the numbing fatigue, they listened intently.

"Then comes a time when you must be careful for your lives. Evil men will drag you before corrupt courts, they will whip you in their synagogues, and you will be hauled before governors and kings for my sake, to bear testimony about me to all nations.

"Don't worry about what to say to them or how to say it. The Holy Spirit will guide you and I will give you such wisdom and eloquence that none of your enemies will be able to contradict a single word.

"But for the rest of the world, brother will betray brother to the death, and fathers their children, and children will betray their fathers. And you will be hated by all—for my name's sake.

"During those horrific days, many believers will fall away. Some will even betray other believers. A host of false prophets will arise and lead others away from the true light. And, because evil rules unchecked, men's love will grow cold.

"But he who endures to the end will be saved. And the gospel of the kingdom will be preached throughout the whole world, as a testimony to the nations. And then—and only then—will the end come."

A particularly stout wind blew out most of the torches, leaving only Judas's torch sputtering weakly. It cast grotesque shadows and the twelve huddled closer together, as much for protection as warmth.

"Is...is there more, Teacher?" Thomas asked, his voice strangely hollow and strained.

"Yes. When you see Jerusalem surrounded by armies, when you see the desolating sacrilege established in the high holy place, then flee to the mountains immediately. Wherever you are, drop everything and run! For these are the days of vengeance.

"I feel sorry for those who are pregnant or who are carrying infants in those days. Pray that your flight will not take place in the dead of winter! For in the days that follow, there will be such a tribulation as has not been seen since the dawn of time. And, if those days were to last long enough, no one would survive. But, for God's chosen ones, there will be an ending. And Jerusalem will be leveled."

John spoke. "Lord, I feel a great fear in my soul, a blackness, a depression like I have never known. Surely a loving God would not destroy virtually the entire human race."

"Ah, John, there is much for you to learn," I said, my own voice filled with a melancholy that the twelve immediately sensed. "I'm afraid there is much, much more.

"After this, men will claim to see the Christ in various places—but don't believe it. For these false Christs and prophets will suddenly appear and be able to perform signs and wonders so amazing that they may even lead some believers astray. But I've warned you of all of this beforehand—so be ever vigilant.

"If they say, 'He is in the wilderness!' or 'He is in the inner rooms!'—don't believe them and don't go! For just as the lightning flashes and lights up the sky from the east to the west, so it will be with the coming of the Son of Man.

"A period of chaos will follow. The moon and sun will darken, stars will fall from heaven, the seas will leave their beds, and the powers of heaven and earth will be shaken.

"Only then will the sign of the Son of Man appear, coming in a great cloud, surrounded by power and glory and the hosts of heaven. And his angels will blow their trumpets to call all believers, from the four corners of the world, on the four winds, and from one end of heaven to another."

Simon had managed to relight some of the torches. What they illuminated were some of the most miserable, exhausted, frightened human beings on the face of the earth. I wanted to hold them all, to assure them that everything would be all right. But I couldn't. At least not yet. This was too important in the telling.

"Now, when all of these things take place, look up! Raise your heads! Because your time of redemption is drawing near!

"Think, for a moment, of the fig tree. As soon as its branches begin to leaf, you know that the summer is near. So it will be when you see these signs. The kingdom is very near. You are at the very gates themselves.

"In fact, this generation will not pass away until all of this has taken place. Heaven and earth may pass away, but my words will not perish.

"And as for when all of this will take place, no one knows. Not the angels. Not the Son. Only our heavenly Father."

We continued our journey after that, a pitiful procession, lit by a handful of faltering torches, stumbling the final mile to Bethany in the pitch blackness of the Judean night.

At last, as we saw the lights of Bethany, Matthew broke the long silence.

"Jesus, is that all we are to know?"

"No, there is something more. Be careful not to waste your time—be it in anxiety, sloth, or drunkenness—because that awful day will close like a trap. It will come on all of those who live on the face of the earth. Always be on watch and pray that you may be able to escape all that is about to happen. And, more importantly, that you will be able to stand before the Son of Man."

But when we finally arrived in Bethany, there were only eleven. Some time during the course of the evening, Judas had slipped away. To where and why, I could only speculate.

But I feared for the worst.

TWO PARABLES OF THE KINGDOM

We stayed in Bethany all of Wednesday. Only Matthew and Simon went into Jerusalem. We were beginning to worry about the safety of Martha, Mary, and Lazarus, even in Bethany, and it was imperative that we find other accommodations.

But when the two returned that evening, Matthew said privately that Simon soon left him on a mission of his own. Searching, no doubt, for Judas.

The remaining disciples were still discussing what I had told them about the final days and the kingdom of heaven. Finally, they came to me and Peter asked me, once again, to describe the kingdom of heaven.

"It is like ten maidens who took their lamps and went to meet the bridegroom," I said.

But before I could finish, Peter turned and beamed at Andrew: "You owe me a copper coin! I *told* you he would answer with a parable!"

Andrew instead threw his sandal at Peter. "Aw, sit down and be quiet. *Some* of us want to hear this."

Let them have their fun, I mused, *there will be precious little time for it in the days to come.*

"*As* I was saying," I continued, "ten maidens awaited the bridegroom. But only five of these maidens were wise—the other five were foolish. And, unlike the wise maidens, the foolish maidens took no extra oil for their lamps. And when the bridegroom was delayed, the ten all fell asleep waiting.

"About midnight, someone shouted, 'The bridegroom is arriving! Come out and meet him!' All ten maidens rose and trimmed their lamps. But the foolish said to the wise, 'Please give us some of your oil, for our lamps are going out.' But the wise replied, 'We're afraid there will not be enough for us and you both. You'd probably better go to the merchants and buy some more for yourselves.'

"And while the foolish maidens were searching for merchants at midnight, the bridegroom arrived and the five who were ready for him went to the lavish wedding feast, shutting and bolting the door behind them.

"Later, when the five foolish maidens returned, they stood outside the door and shouted 'Lord! Lord! Open to us!'

"But the bridegroom replied, 'I'm afraid I don't know you.' "

I stopped and looked at those assembled.

"Who knows what the message to that parable is? Nathanael?"

Nathanael jumped slightly, creased his brow a moment and finally said, "I'm not sure. Uhh, that five maidens is plenty for any sane man?"

Suddenly, a host of dusty sandals flew across the room, all striking Nathanael at once.

"No!" I shouted, even as a one-sided sandal fight erupted in earnest. "The moral is: watch carefully—for you know neither the day nor the hour!"

THE LAST SUPPER

On Thursday morning, we continued resting and began our preparations for the Passover and the Feast of Unleavened Bread. Still no sign of Judas.

About midday, two men came and met briefly with Simon. When they'd left, he took me to the roof.

"We must leave Bethany now, Lord," Simon said. "It is no longer safe here."

"Then we will go into Jerusalem and search for a place to stay and eat the Passover meal."

We said our good-byes, for the last time, to Mary, Martha, and Lazarus.

For once, with the massive crowds flooding into Jerusalem for Passover, we were able to steal into the Holy City without drawing undue notice—and unwelcome attention. We still didn't have a place to eat the Passover meal, though Matthew continued to scour the city for a safe haven.

At last, I prayed about it, then I called Peter and John over.

"Go into the Upper City. You will shortly encounter a man carrying a water jug. Follow him. And when he goes into a house, say to the owner, 'The Teacher says to you, "Where is the guest room where I am to eat the Passover with my disciples?"' And he will show you a large upper room, furnished and ready for the meal."

Nodding, they left.

An hour passed.

During that time, Judas returned, Simon close at his side—perhaps *too* close. Judas refused to speak where he'd been. But, from that moment on, Simon was his constant shadow.

Eventually, Peter and John returned as well.

"It was as you said," Peter said. "It is not far from the house of Caiaphas, hard by the Essene Gate."

As we walked the back roads and alleys, Simon quickly filled us in on what he'd seen and heard.

"We can't spend the night in Jerusalem either," he said, never taking his eyes off Judas. "Our friends' spies are out in force. There is a healthy bounty for our capture."

"Then where *will* we spend the night?" Matthew, ever the stickler for details, asked.

"About all I could find that I know is safe are some sheltered eves in a garden called Gethsemane on the Mount of Olives," Simon answered. "I've had some blankets sent there; it will do for the night. Plus it is secluded and off the beaten track—with only one entrance to guard."

"Thank you for your hard work," I said. "I know of the place. It is very beautiful."

By taking Simon's winding route, we arrived at the proper location after nearly an hour's walk. Our meeting place was a large, otherwise nondescript, second-floor room. The owner's servants prepared the meal to our specifications, then withdrew. As we reclined around the banqueting table, I said, "Truly, one of you tonight, one of you eating this very meal with me, will betray me."

An excited hubbub went up from the twelve. At last, Peter cried, "Lord, is it I?" Then the others followed, asking the same question.

"One of you who is dipping his bread with me tonight will betray me," I repeated quietly, still getting used to the idea. "The Son of Man will go and do as it is written about him. But I feel sorry for the man who betrays the Son of Man! Perhaps it would be better if he were never born."

Judas leaned over and hissed through clenched teeth, "Surely you're not talking about me, Rabbi."

Our eyes met and locked.

"You yourself have said it."

Judas looked away.

I spoke to the twelve:

"I have prayed that I would have the opportunity to eat this Passover with you before I suffer. For I shall not eat again it until it is fulfilled in the kingdom of heaven."

I took a piece of bread, blessed it and broke it, and gave it to the twelve, saying, "Take and eat—for this is my body, broken for you."

After we had eaten, I took the cup, gave thanks, and passed it to each man in turn, saying, "Drink of it, all of you, for this is my blood of the covenant, which is poured out for many—for the forgiveness of sins. Truly, I shall not drink again of the fruit of the vine until that day when I drink it new, with you, in my Father's kingdom."

It was a lovely, bittersweet moment. Lit by the flickering candles, I sat quietly with the twelve for long moments, drinking it in. I loved them all—even Judas. They had sacrificed and dared much for me in the previous three years.

Then I got up, shed my outer garments, wrapped a towel around my waist, poured water in a basin, and began washing their feet, drying them with my towel.

But Peter pulled his feet back.

"Lord, you're not really going to wash my feet, are you?"

"You don't realize now what I'm doing, but later—perhaps much later—you will understand, my friend."

"No! I won't do it. *You* won't do it!" he said. "You will never wash my feet."

"Peter," I said softly, "unless I wash your feet tonight, you will have no part with me."

Peter fell to the floor beside me. "Then, Lord, wash not just my feet like some slave, but wash my hands and my head as well!"

"A person who has had a bath needs only to wash his feet—his whole body is clean. And you, my friend..." I cupped his chin in my hand "...are clean. Though not all of you here tonight are so clean."

Then I dressed and returned to my place. "Do you understand what I have done for you?" I asked them. "You call me 'Teacher' and 'Lord,' and rightly so, for that is exactly what I am. But now that I—your Lord and teacher—have washed your feet, you should wash one another's feet. I have set an example for you, so you will do as I have done. I tell you the truth: no servant is greater than his master, nor is a messenger greater than the one who sent him. And now that you know these things, you will be forever blessed if you follow them."

The twelve continued to stare at me. A few, with full comprehension dawning in their eyes. Others, with only slivers of the truth to digest. Still others were a long way from understanding what they had seen and heard. And one...

"I am not referring to all of you, I'm afraid," I continued. "I know those I chose, but one of you has fulfilled the Scripture, 'He who shares my bread has lifted up his heel against me.'

"I'm telling you this now, before it happens, so that when it actually takes place, you will believe that I am He. Again:

Whoever accepts anyone I send, accepts me. Anyone who accepts me, accepts the One who sent me."

Again, the disciples began discussing among themselves what I said about a traitor in their midst. For the remaining eleven, it was inconceivable that someone who had endured all they'd endured, seen all they'd seen, heard all they'd heard, could possibly betray me. And for the twelfth, it was all *too* possible.

Finally, Peter leaned over to John, who was sitting next to me, and whispered, "Go on—ask him who he is talking about—the suspense is killing me!"

John did just that:

"Lord, who *is* it?"

"It is as I have said before, the one to whom I have been dipping this bread is the one," I said.

With that, I dipped a crust of bread in the olive oil, then handed it to Judas Iscariot, the son of Simon.

He reached for it by instinct, then drew back his hand.

Then he looked at me.

His eyes were filled with messianic dreams, of messiahs on white chargers, routing the enemies of Israel. His eyes were filled with hopes unfulfilled, of dreams undreamed, of goals unmet. His eyes were filled with pain and sorrow and humiliation.

His eyes were filled with betrayal.

His hand shook as he took the crust, then he flung it across the room.

"What you have to do, Judas, do quickly," I said.

Then Judas rushed from the room.

Simon started up to follow him, but I shook my head.

Reluctantly, Simon returned to the table, although he continued to eye me curiously.

At the end of the table, Thomas turned to Little James.

"Where's *Judas* going?"

"Oh, I dunno. Probably out to buy what we need for the feast. Or maybe to give something to the poor. Who cares about that Judean? He's a cold fish at the best of times."

With Judas gone, an oppressive weight was lifted from my shoulders.

"And so, my friends," I said, "the time has come for us to talk, as plainly as I know how.

"Now is the Son of Man glorified—and God glorified in him. For I will be with you only a little while longer. You will look for me but—just as I told the Judeans once before—where I am going, you can't go.

"Tonight, I'm giving you a new commandment: Love one another. As I have loved you, you must love one another. By this, all men and women will know that you are my disciples."

Peter asked, "Lord, just where *are* you going?"

"Where I am going, you cannot follow for now. But, someday, you will follow me there."

Peter looked indignant at first, then hurt.

"Why *can't* I follow you now? I will lay down my life for you right now!"

I gazed at his broad, honest face, his ruddy cheeks, and his short, curly beard. Peter had more than once placed his life on the line for me. But not this time.

"Will you really, Peter? Will you really lay your life down for me?" I asked. "In truth, before the rooster crows tomorrow morning, you will deny me three times!"

"Never!" he shouted. "Lord, I..."

But I motioned for him to listen.

"Do not let your hearts be troubled," I told the eleven. "Trust in God. Trust also in me. In my Father's house, there are many rooms. If this were not so, I promise I would have told you so long before now. Shortly, I am…I am going there to prepare a place for each of you. And, in time, I will come back and take you to be with me so that we'll always be together. You—all of you—know the way to the place where I am going."

Thomas suddenly pounded the table in exasperation. "No! No, Lord, we *don't* know where you are going. *None* of us know—so how can we know the way?!"

"Thomas, *I* am the way. *I* am the truth. *I* am the life. *No one* comes to the Father except through me. If you *really* knew me, you'd know my Father as well. And, from this moment forward, you *do* know him—*and have seen him!*"

And then we left, singing a hymn, a joyous, celebratory hymn, the second half of *The Hallel*.

I know what is ahead. It is all the more reason to sing a song of celebration. I know of the pain and horror ahead. All the more reason to sing a song of hope.

There is, my Father, a joy deeper than sorrow.

Help me to remember it in the hours ahead.

GETHSEMANE

We walked through the quiet, cobbled side streets of Jerusalem, utterly alone, save for the passing sentry or nightwatchman. It seemed that Simon knew every back alley and shortcut in Jerusalem—and we needed them all to get out of the city undetected.

Then, following the light of a single torch, we made our way to the Garden of Gethsemane. As promised, there were enough blankets for all of us, even in the chilly March air.

The eleven shuffled along blindly, more asleep than awake. But my mind was on fire with all that I knew was coming. There would be no sleep for me tonight.

Once at Gethsemane, I asked Peter, John, and Big James to accompany me further into the garden.

"My soul is full of sorrow, even unto death," I told them privately. "Please, remain with me a little while longer, and watch and pray with me."

I walked a few feet away, knelt by a boulder, and prayed, "Father, all things are possible for you. Please, take this bitter cup from me if there's any other way. But if there is not, then may your will be done—not mine."

After a while, I looked back. Peter, John, and Big James were all fast asleep.

Still tormented and fighting a monstrous, all-consuming depression, I went to them.

"So, you could not watch with me—for even one more hour. Pray that you won't be tempted. I know the spirit is willing, but the flesh is weak."

Peter made a big show of slapping himself in the face, beating his arms about his body, and sitting erect to watch while I finished my prayers.

I withdrew and prayed the same agonizing prayer. And when I looked back, all three were slumped together, sleeping like babies.

I went to them, roused them, and begged them a third time to watch and pray with me. I felt so terribly alone. But this time, even Peter could only sleepily agree to watch.

My third and final prayer was sheer torture. I flung myself on the ground, begging my Father that his perfect will be done. I was in such torment that I began to sweat blood.

But the answer was the same every time.

The cup would not—could not—pass from me.

And so, shaking and feverish, I walked back to the three. All were sleeping soundly.

I reluctantly woke them one last time.

"Are you still sleeping and taking your rest?" I asked them gently. "I'm afraid your rest is finished. The time has come, the hour is at hand.

"The Son of Man is betrayed."

At that moment, I heard a great commotion outside the garden. Through the trees, I could see a long line of torches, streaming up the mountain, stretching all the way back to Jerusalem. I could hear angry, dangerous voices.

The noise woke the remaining eight. But in their still-groggy state, they reacted slowly, if at all.

Then the procession burst into the Garden of Gethsemane. At its head was Judas! Behind him were some of the most virulent priests, elders, scribes, Pharisees, and Sadducees we'd encountered in our days in Jerusalem.

They plowed through our little band like a Roman phalanx, sending still-befuddled disciples tumbling in all directions. Simon drew his sword, but was quickly overpowered by a half-dozen heavily armed men.

Judas separated himself from the others and walked up to me. He said loudly, "Hail, Master!" and kissed me on the cheek.

I held him briefly in my arms and whispered, "Judas, why would you choose a kiss as your instrument of betrayal?"

With that kiss, a number of men pulled their swords and rushed me. Peter knocked me aside, grabbed Judas's sword, and slashed at our attackers. A muscular slave howled in pain, his ear severed cleanly off.

I lunged between Peter and the other armed men.

"Peter, put that sword away!" I shouted angrily. "Don't you know that all who take the sword will perish by the sword? And don't you think that I could—if I wanted to—call to my Father and he'd surround me with twelve legions of angels?! No more of this!"

I reached down, plucked the bleeding ear from the rocky ground, and reattached it to the head of the dazed and incredulous slave.

Then I turned to the mob. "Have you come out against me as a robber, with your swords and clubs drawn, to capture me? Day after day, I sat in the Temple teaching—and you did not seize me then.

"But all of you here tonight, remember this: everything that has happened is accomplished that the Scriptures might be fulfilled. But this, my friends, is your hour.

"And the hour of the power of darkness."

With that, my disciples disappeared into the night, fleeing in every direction. One was briefly captured, but managed to escape, leaving only his cloak and tunic behind in their hands.

And I was led, bound and tethered, down into Jerusalem below.

CHAPTER EIGHT

The Final Ordeal

THE SANHEDRIN TRIAL

The torch-lit journey from the Garden of Gethsemane into Jerusalem had a nightmarish, unreal quality about it. It was conducted in complete silence, save only the clattering of the Roman scabbards on their armor. I never saw Judas again.

As we walked the streets of the Holy City, occasionally I'd see someone peeking from behind a closed window. I thought I caught glimpses of Simon and Peter, running furtively along parallel courses, following our procession, but I couldn't be sure.

At last we came to a richly appointed mansion in the southern sector of the Upper City, not far from the theater, though I couldn't be sure in the dark.

Waiting inside were more priests and officials, including Annas, the brother-in-law of Caiaphas, and—according to Simon—the true power behind the throne. The rest I wasn't sure about, but there appeared to be a number of Sadducees.

They shoved me before Annas, a fat, oily-looking man with a permanent sneer, and a number of other priests and scribes, all sitting behind a table. They immediately began questioning me about my disciples and my teachings. And, as before, the questions were designed to trick me into admitting some imagined heresy or another.

I patiently answered every question until at last I said, "I have always spoken openly. I always taught in the synagogues or at the Temple or in the open marketplaces where all Jews come together. I've said nothing in secret. Why question me now?"

I pointed to several familiar faces. "Ask one of them—they all heard me speak numerous times. They know what I've said."

With that, a man in Annas's entourage wheeled back and struck me in the face, snapping my head back, and knocking me to the floor. He stood over me and snarled, "Is this the way you answer a high priest?"

Since my hands were bound, it was difficult to regain my feet. With blood running down my face, I looked squarely at Annas and said, "If I've said something wrong, tell me—and all those assembled here—what it was. But if I spoke the truth, why did you strike me?"

Annas conferred briefly with the Sadducees, who shrugged their shoulders.

"Send him on to Caiaphas," Annas barked.

I was roughly yanked and pulled out the door. As we walked through Annas's spacious courtyard, I saw a number of people warming themselves around small fires. It was difficult to tell in the glimmering half-light, but I was sure I saw John and, perhaps, Peter.

Caiaphas lived nearby in an even more expansive home. It was well lit and teeming with activity. But as we walked along the street, those holding me began hissing curses and threats, striking me repeatedly. Then, as we waited in the courtyard to be summoned before Caiaphas, they blindfolded me. Suddenly, several of them began beating me, all the while whispering, "Prophesy! Who struck you *that* time, Nazarene?"

Finally, when I was dragged inside, I was surprised to see many of the Sanhedrin in attendance—but *not* Nicodemus or Joseph of Arimathea. Perhaps Caiaphas only wanted those present whose votes he could count on.

He convened an obscene mockery of a court, calling numerous witnesses, mostly men I'd never seen before, expertly shaping the questions so that they'd testify that I'd said something blasphemous or traitorous. But their paid witnesses were so inept that they couldn't agree even on the simplest lie.

Finally, two frightened-looking merchants were dragged forward. Caiaphas hounded them mercilessly, badgering them with questions. At last, the smaller of the two men said, in a barely audible voice, "We, uh, heard him say that he, uh, will destroy the entire Temple in three days."

Then the other chimed in, "Yeah, then he said he'd rebuild it in another three days. I think."

Many of the members of the Sanhedrin laughed, yet Caiaphas took the wobbly testimony seriously.

"You've heard the damning testimony against you, Jesus!" he roared. "After all this, what do you have to say in your so-called defense? What about this threat to destroy our beloved Temple?"

But whatever answer I made would only give them more "evidence" against me. I stared straight ahead, my left eye beginning to swell shut from the beating.

This infuriated Caiaphas. He bounded down from his high seat, and stood directly in front of me screaming, "I adjure you by the Living God! Tell us if you are the Christ, the Son of God!"

I licked my split lips and said, as clearly as I could, "I am. And you will see the Son of Man sitting at the right hand of Power, coming with the clouds of heaven."

Caiaphas howled like a dying dog, covered his ears, then threw himself to the floor, writhing around like a man in his death throes. After a few seconds, he jumped back up and began dramatically tearing at his clothes, still howling.

"Blasphemer! He has spoken blasphemy! We don't need anymore witnesses—you have all heard it! What is your judgment on this demon?!"

Caiaphas pointed at each member of the Sanhedrin present and each member shouted "Death!" A few rushed up and spit on me and others surged forward to claw my face and beat me until Caiaphas finally broke it up.

He called the other Pharisee leaders together.

"As you know, we can't actually condemn this fool to death—only Pilate can do that," Caiaphas said expansively. "But I think you will find Pilate...cooperative. After all, he needed our support—and financing from the Temple funds—when he wanted to build Jerusalem's aqueduct, didn't he?"

The others nodded wisely, stroking their well-groomed beards.

"Good. Now take him away."

I was dragged off again, out through the courtyard, and into the night. Again, I thought I saw Peter standing on the fringes of one of the fires, but his face was buried in his hands and he appeared to be weeping, so I couldn't be sure.

Somewhere in the courtyard, a cock was crowing.

FIRST APPEARANCE BEFORE PILATE

Dawn was breaking as I was dragged, sometimes pulled, over the cobbled streets. Pilate's palace and judgment hall were located

on the extreme northern side of Jerusalem, near the Temple, in what
is called the Second Quarter. But the Jews with me didn't want to
become ceremonially unclean, so they sent messengers in asking
Pilate if he would meet them outside, on the steps of the palace.

After a long wait, Pilate came out, only half-dressed, obviously
angry over being awaken.

"All right, all right," he grumbled, "what charges are you people bringing against this man?"

The chief elder stepped forward and said, "Governor, we
found this wretch trying to overthrow our nation. He urged
others to withhold their lawful taxes to Caesar. And he claims
that he is the long-awaited Christ—the king of the Jews."

Pilate laughed a short, nasty laugh. "Okay, little man, are you
really the king of the Jews?"

"You have said so," I replied. "Did you know that—or did
others tell you first?"

That stirred up a hornet's nest! All of the priests and Pharisees
immediately began shouting other accusations at me.

Pilate listened for a minute, then contemptuously cut them off.

"You! The accused!" he said. "What do you say to all of these
amazing charges from your own people?"

Most were so spurious, so silly, that any sane man could have
seen through them.

I answered, "My kingdom is not of this world. If it were, my
servants would be fighting to prevent my arrest by the Jews. But
now, my kingdom is in another place, far, far from here."

"So you *are* a king!" Pilate exclaimed proudly, as if he'd
unlocked some timeless riddle.

"Yes, you're right—I am a king," I said. "For this I was born
into this world—to testify the truth. And everyone who believes
in the truth listens to me."

Pilate laughed again and threw up his hands.

"What *is* truth, little man?"

Then, to the priests, "I find no fault in this man, no crime."

But Caiaphas himself stepped forward, his eyes blazing.

"Oh, great governor, this pathetic Galilean is inciting the people to revolution against Rome, from Judea to Galilee—even to Jerusalem."

"Oh, so he's a Galilean!" Pilate said, obviously enjoying Caiaphas's discomfort. "Then he's not my problem, is he? Galilee, of course, is in Herod's jurisdiction, Caiaphas. Or don't you know your geography, either?"

Pilate looked back over his shoulder. A spectacularly beautiful woman with exotic red hair was leaning out the window, beckoning to him. Pilate then looked peevishly back at Caiaphas.

"I've got important business to attend to today, Caiaphas. Take this Galilean to Herod."

With that, he walked briskly back into his palace.

APPEARANCE BEFORE HEROD

I could see Caiaphas seething with anger.

He yapped at his priests and attendants, "He is doing this just to torment me! Pilate and Herod hate each other. But I don't see that we have any other choice. Send messengers ahead to Herod, we will see him immediately."

Once again I was half-pulled, half-dragged across Jerusalem in the dawn's early light. Herod's incredible palace was not far, near the western wall, by the Gennath Gate.

Herod himself was waiting to meet us. Herod wore a glittering array of silk and linen robes, heavily embroidered and inlaid with precious stones. He spoke with a thin, reedy voice and he clapped his hands as I approached.

"Oh, Jesus of Nazareth! I've heard so much about you! Your fame precedes you, even in my humble house. Please, just for me, do a sign or miracle. Just a small one."

I looked straight at him, but didn't answer.

Herod's whimsical demeanor vanished. He began questioning me, using the same questions asked earlier by the Sadducees and Pharisees.

Again, I had no answers for their leading questions.

They will have their way with me, one way or the other, I thought.

In exasperation, the priests and scribes began vehemently attacking and accusing me.

At last, Herod threw up his dainty, bejeweled hands and trilled to his heavily armed guards, "Do with him as you please. He's hopeless."

Several of Herod's guards smiled sadistic smiles and walked forward, then began to painfully, methodically beat me, smashing blow after blow into my back and sides.

After a few blood-spattered seconds, Herod grew bored with the spectacle.

"Enough. Galilean or not, he's Pilate's problem since this so-called messiah has been stirring up unrest here in Jerusalem. But Caiaphas, please extend to Pilate my thanks for letting me finally meet this 'silent' king. It was almost a thrill."

I knelt in front of Herod, bleeding and battered, still staring at him, my clothes shredded and blood-soaked.

"Oh, dear Jesus, you'll catch your death of cold in that tacky outfit," Herod giggled. He grandly swept off one of his lovely robes and had it draped around my shoulders.

"There! Now you'll look nice when you see Pontius Pilate. Good-bye, king of the Jews!"

Second Appearance Before Pilate

This time, crowds were beginning to gather in the streets, even at this early hour. Soon a large procession was following us back to Pilate's palace.

Pilate was even less eager to see me a second time, but finally he emerged, fully dressed, from his palace. After a long, animated discussion with Caiaphas, he stepped forward to address the crowd.

"I still find no basis for a charge of treason against this man," he shouted to the assembled multitude. "And neither did Herod—since he sent him back to me. You can't put a man to death for no reason. But if it'll make you happy, I'll have him whipped, then you can have him back."

But the crowd, led by the priests and Pharisees, began shouting, "No! No! No! Kill him! Kill him!"

Clearly taken aback, Pilate conferred briefly with one of his advisors. The advisor sent a messenger off at a dead run.

"It's our royal custom, at the time of your Passover, to release one prisoner to you," he boomed to the crowd. "This year, however, I'll give you a choice. You can either have this Jesus released, or you can have Barabbas."

This silenced the crowd. Barabbas was known to be a violent man and a casual murderer. But even that didn't stop the scribes and Pharisees. The chant quickly began, "Barabbas! Barabbas! Barabbas!"

Pilate laughed his unpleasant laugh again. "All right, you fools, it's Barabbas's tender mercies you'll have among you again, stalking your precious women and children.

"So. What shall I do with the king of the Jews?"

"Crucify him! Crucify him! Crucify him!"

All my dreams, all my visions, all my portents into the future—they've always pointed to a Roman crucifixion.

"Crucify him?" Pilate was plainly astonished. "An innocent man? My, you *are* a bloodthirsty lot this morning."

But the chant continued, unabated.

Pilate now appeared to be somewhat alarmed. The little scenario that had been amusing him was turning deadly.

He motioned for Caiaphas to approach him.

"You do whatever your arcane laws require, priest—but there is no basis for crucifixion and outright murder here."

Caiaphas whined, "We have a law, oh governor. And, according to that holy law, this man must die because he claims to be the Son of God."

Pilate swore mightily at Caiaphas, then had me brought inside the palace, out of earshot of the mob.

"Listen, little man," he hissed. "Where do you come from?"

But I didn't answer.

"You fool—you refuse to speak to me? Don't you realize that I'm the only one who has the power to free you or crucify you? Do you have a death wish?"

I could barely see out of my left eye and my mouth was so battered and bruised, it was painful to talk. But I raised my face to his and said, "You would have no power over me if it were not given to you from above, Pilate. Therefore, the man who handed me over to you is guilty of a greater sin."

Pilate threw up his hands in a gesture of hopelessness. Then he led me back outside where Caiaphas was waiting.

Caiaphas was now clearly infuriated. "If you free this criminal, you are no friend of Caesar! Anyone who claims to be king is Caesar's enemy!" And, in a voice so low only the three of us heard it, "And I personally will see to it that Caesar hears of your behavior, if you let this traitorous would-be king free."

Pilate and Caiaphas glared at each other for long seconds, then Pilate called for his judgment seat. When it was brought outside, he sat on it and had me dragged to his side.

"Here is your king!" he shouted to the mob.

"Crucify him! Crucify him!" the howls began anew.

Pilate looked at them in mock astonishment.

"What? Me? Crucify your king?"

"We have no king but Caesar!" they shouted. "Crucify him! CRUCIFY HIM!"

Pilate sighed a long, dramatic sigh, waved a hand for quiet, then motioned to one of his attendants. The servant brought a basin of water forward. He began washing his hands in front of them.

"This is to show publicly that I am innocent of this man's blood. See to it yourselves."

Caiaphas smiled a twisted smile at Pilate as he bowed deeply. "His blood will be on us and our children, my lord."

Pilate's look was one of unadulterated hate.

"Oh, and don't forget your friend Barabbas, Caiaphas. I place him in your personal supervision."

The soldiers brought Barabbas, beaten and bleeding himself, forward and thrust him roughly at Caiaphas's feet.

But as Barabbas passed, he glanced wildly at me, obviously not comprehending what was going on.

"Be at peace, my friend," I whispered.

Obviously disgusted by the entire sordid spectacle, Pilate turned to his soldiers. "Now scourge this hopeless madman Jesus. Crucifixion is bad enough—a good scourge is a mercy. It'll shorten his misery on the cross. Then give him back to the Jews. And I don't want to hear any more about it. Ever!"

THE CRUCIFIXION

The Roman soldiers dragged me back inside the palace to their barracks. Someone took Herod's beautiful, though now badly bloodstained, robe from me and replaced it with a red one.

Then they whipped me with fragments of iron tied to strips of leather. Within a few blows, my entire back was laid open and raw before them. Each strike exposed new nerve endings and shredded bits of muscle.

I prayed frantically for strength, for patience, for courage.

When the whipping was done—or, more likely, they were bored with it—a few of the soldiers threw me against a wall. One smashed a crown of thorns on my head; another soldier stuck a reed in my hand. Then they pretended to bow before me, chanting "Hail! King of the Jews!"

Others wandered up and halfheartedly spit upon me and beat me, but I was barely able to keep my head erect by now, so there was little sport in it.

At last, they dragged me outside. A carpenter had made three rude crosses. They gave me one, then led me back onto the streets of Jerusalem. The mob was waiting for us, screeching their insults and hatred. I was already so weak from the beatings and loss of blood that I could barely lift the heavy wooden cross. I walked a few feet, then stumbled under its weight.

After this happened several times, the soldiers reached into the crowd lining the streets and grabbed a strapping young man.

"You!" the old soldier grunted. "What's your name?"

"Uh, my name is Simon. I'm a Cyrene," he croaked, shaking with fear.

"Well, Simon the Cyrene, you're going to carry the king of the Jews's cross."

"Where...where are we going?"

"Just outside the First and Second Walls, country-boy, to a hill called Golgotha."

So they dumped the cross on Simon's back and our pitiful procession continued. It was now about eight o'clock in the morning.

Though the sweat and blood stained my eyes, I kept catching glimpses of people I knew in the crowd. Some had been there to welcome me into Jerusalem, just days before. Some were Pharisees. Some were followers of John the Baptist. I thought I saw Simon the Zealot once. I was sure I saw Peter and John as we approached the gates. Mary Magdalene lifted a hand toward me.

Just outside the Gennath Gate, by the Tower's Pool, we passed a large group of women. All were shocked at my brutalized appearance, all were weeping and wailing and lamenting my fate.

Through cracked and bleeding lips, I said to them, "Daughters of Jerusalem, do not cry for me. Weep for yourselves, weep for your children. The day is coming when people will say, 'Blessed are those without children.' They will say to the mountains, 'Fall on us,' and to the hills, 'Cover us'—for if they do this when the wood is green, what will happen when the wood is dry?"

Then we were past them. If I slowed, even to catch my breath, I felt a Roman boot in my ribs or a spear butt in my back.

Behind me were two more unfortunates, both carrying their own crosses, also being herded to the hill called "The Skull."

Once there, they stripped us, threw us down on the our crosses, and the carpenters began the gruesome task of nailing our hands and feet to the splintered wood. The old man was a professional: he expertly drove the spikes between major bones and blood vessels, otherwise death could come in a matter of minutes, not hours or days, like the Romans—and Jews—demanded.

I was so lightheaded from the pain and loss of blood that shuddering hammer-blows scarcely added to my torment.

One of the soldiers produced a sign written in Aramaic, Greek, and Latin, saying "Jesus of Nazareth, king of the Jews." But when he went to nail in the space above my head, fat Annas appeared and stopped him.

"Don't put that up." Annas hissed, "Put, 'This man *claimed* to be the king of the Jews.'"

The soldier shrugged and turned his back on Annas.

"This is what Pilate wrote. This is what he gave me. This is what I nail to the stupid cross."

And he did.

The real pain didn't begin until I was hoisted and slammed into a hastily dug hole in the ground. The skin tore and the bones scraped against the spike as the earth pulled my body down. To breathe, I had to hoist myself up with my arms, but I didn't have the strength to do that for long. And when I slid back down, the wood splintered and tore my already tattered back.

I looked up into the clouded morning sky and said, "Father, forgive them, for they don't know what they're doing."

It was about nine in the morning.

Within minutes, swarms of flies filled the air around us.

The Romans keeping guard then erected the remaining two crosses. More people filtered out of the city to join the crowd already on Golgotha.

The old carpenter apparently took pity on me. He stuck a sponge on the end of a spear, dipped it in a bucket, and lifted it to my lips. It was wine mixed with a mild drug, to numb the pain. I turned away and, with great difficulty, shook my head.

The long minutes stretched into long hours. The Roman soldiers kept a strong perimeter around the three crosses, but the mob had swollen to the point that it surrounded us on all sides. Through the haze of pain, I could hear the slurs and epithets hurled by those watching my ordeal:

"Ha! You're the one who'll destroy the Temple and rebuild it in three days? Save yourself, man!"

"If you really are the Son of God, come down from that cross!"

"You saved others—now save yourself!"

"Come on, king of Israel—now's your chance. If you come down from the cross right now, I'll believe!"

"You trust in God—tell God to save you now, Nazarene!"

From my one good eye, I could see that some of my tormenters were the same scribes, Pharisees, elders, and priests who had dogged my steps for the past three years. They'd come to gloat and jeer and enjoy my suffering. I could pick out Goat-beard and Bald Pharisee at the front of the happy group. But in the back stood Makir—Blue Robe—quiet and unmoving.

I could also see friends and family members scattered through the crowd.

Mother! You've come! I don't know how you knew—but you're here! Don't cry, mother, it will soon pass!

And look! There's my mother's sister. And there's Mary Magdalene and Mary, the wife of Clopas.

I see Peter on the fringes of the crowd. That looks like Simon hiding in the shadows of the tower.

And who's that coming from the back? It's John!

I waited until John was near my mother and tried to speak, but my voice was nearly gone.

"Mother, here is your son," I said to Mary, my voice a grotesque gurgle. And to John, "John, behold, this is your mother."

They embraced and I was gratified to see that John stuck by my mother's side from that point on.

It must have been about eleven o'clock. I could feel myself weakening with every passing hour.

Suddenly, I heard from the man who was hanging on my left. He'd been howling his pain and cursing the Romans for long hours until his voice was little more than a scratchy rasp.

"Aren't you the Christ? Save yourself—and save us!" he said, his voice a mixture of anger and desperation.

But the man on my right spoke to us for the first time as well. He painfully turned his head and looked at the other man. "You must not fear God to speak to this man like that. We deserve what's happening to us—we were caught red-handed. But this man has done nothing. Nothing!"

Then he looked at me, his eyes narrow slits against the pain.

"Jesus," he gasped, "please—remember me when you reach your heavenly kingdom."

I tried to smile as best my misshapened and swollen lips would allow and said to him in a hoarse whisper, "Truly, my friend, today you will join me in Paradise."

I tried to think, to pray, to sing, to do anything—but the pain was the center of my being. It only allowed brief, incomplete thoughts, then overwhelmed them in another wave of pain.

I was aware, however, that as we approached what must have been the noon hour, the clouds continued to gather and darken. And by noon, they were so thick and black, it was difficult to see.

Each heaving breath was torture. I struggled to lift myself up and gulp a few half-swallows of air, then sagged down, grinding the spikes into the muscles and bones of my hand.

There were no more thoughts now.

There was only the pain.

But with each passing moment, more of my life's blood dripped away in a spreading pool at the foot of my twisted cross. The blood was now black. The flow was slowing.

I could still see the mocking groups and some soldiers dividing my blood-soaked garments, casting lots for the odd piece. One of the psalms flashed through my mind, "All who see me mock at me...a company of evildoers encircles me...they divide my garments among themselves and cast lots for my clothing."

And, for the first time in my life, I could not feel my Father's presence.

I summoned my rapidly ebbing strength and in a spray of blood cried out the beginning line of that psalm, "My God! My God! Why have you forsaken me?"

I wanted to say more, but that was all I was able to croak out. My throat was parched and I was dehydrated from loss of blood.

Another soldier, apparently a veteran of these crucifixions, saw me trying to speak and figured out my problem. He dipped another sponge in a bowl of sour wine, jabbed it on a long reed, and held it up.

But before it reached my lips, the other soldiers said, "Wait! Let's see if this Elijah will save him first!"

But the old soldier knocked them aside and dribbled a little on my lips.

It was enough.

I looked at them all one last time in the gathering darkness, Pharisees and friends, family members and followers, Roman soldiers, scribes, priests, the idly curious, the sympathetic women from Jerusalem.

Then I forced my head upward.

"My Father, into your hands I commit my soul."

In that instant, the blackness on all sides of me came rushing toward me, like I was a stone thrown in a black ocean.

My last words were, "It is finished."

And I knew no more but pain.

Mother, tell me the story again...

And blackness.

...about the three wise kings from the East...

And hopelessness.

...who gave you this beautiful gold coin...

And despair.

...the smells of the caravan...

And the sin of the world smothering me, filling me, drowning me, covering me in black.

...the star that night...

Black.

A New Beginning

THE BURIAL

J oseph, there's someone at the door."

Joseph's blood froze.

They've come for me now. First Jesus, now his followers.

"Oh, Joseph, I wish we'd never left Arimathea," Tirzah wailed.

"Be brave, my love," he said.

As bravely as Jesus died, then we must be as brave, whatever is to come.

He opened the door.

But instead of a platoon of heavily armed Roman soldiers, there stood a single woman, Mary of Magdala.

"Mary! You startled me! Please come in, come in."

Tirzah rushed to hug Mary.

"Oh, you've been crying, my friend," Tirzah said. "But then, after the events of the last few hours, I suppose half of Jerusalem is crying. Let me get you something to drink."

In front of the fire, cupping her drink, Mary sat staring at the crackling flames.

"Mary," Joseph asked softly, "were you there?"

"From the moment I heard he'd been arrested, to the moment he said, 'It is finished.' "

"We left," Joseph said, as if ashamed. "What happened after that?"

"Caiaphas told the guard that since it is the day of Preparation, he didn't want to defile the High Holy Day by having those bodies still hanging there outside the walls. So he'd secured permission from Pilate to have them taken down. Caiaphas then told the soldiers to...to break their legs and drag them down. The other two were still alive—barely. One had gone mad. He tore himself free, and was still whimpering at the foot of his cross! The soldiers took care of them both in the usual efficient Roman manner."

"And Jesus?" Tirzah asked.

"But Jesus was already dead," Mary said in a monotone. "So one of the soldiers, just to be sure, I guess, sta...stabbed him in the side with his spear. He...he never moved.

"I have no more tears."

"Anything more?"

"One thing, it seemed that just as Jesus died, the earth moved. But perhaps I imagined it."

"No," Tirzah cried—"we felt it too, here in town!"

"Some strange, fantastic rumors have been shooting through the city in the last couple of hours," Joseph said. "There are reports that the earthquake shook open some tombs and that some corpses have reanimated.

"And there's more." Joseph dropped his voice to a conspiratorial whisper. "A friend of mine in the Temple tells me that about three o'clock, the curtain in the Holy of Holies split in two! From ceiling to floor!"

Mary gasped. "That's when Jesus died!"

"Naturally, the Pharisees and priests have been working overtime in the last few hours, trying to stamp out these reports. They're even arresting anyone who repeats one of these stories."

"These are bad days, Mary, bad days," Tirzah said. "Have you heard about Judas?"

"Only that he sold out our Lord for thirty pieces of silver."

"There's more," Joseph said. "He was found this afternoon—also about three o'clock. Matthew said he hanged himself."

"I'm not surprised. But I just remembered something else that happened following the earthquake."

Joseph said, "Please, tell us. It is important that you remember everything."

"The soldiers had been gradually relaxing their watch around the crucifixion. So when the earthquake immediately followed Jesus' last words, I was actually pretty close to him. There was a centurion standing guard as well. He was knocked to his feet. He looked at Jesus, then looked at me and Maariah, and said, "Truly, this was the Son of God! Truly, this man was innocent!""

Mary took a long draught of her warm drink.

"What of the others, Mary?" Tirzah asked. "What of the remaining disciples?"

"Scattered like the wind," Mary said. "Caiaphas and Annas particularly want Peter and Simon, but they'll never find them. And if they do, they'll never take Simon alive."

Tirzah shuddered at the thought.

"Mary, we are delighted that you are here," Joseph said carefully. "But it is not safe for you to be about. Why have you come?"

"I was contacted just a little while ago by Nicodemus. He thinks it better that the two of you not be seen together, Joseph. Nicodemus says that you have influence with Pilate. He begs you to ask Pilate for Jesus' body. He has all of the necessary burial strips, herbs, and spices. There...there isn't much time before the Sabbath."

Mary looked away from the fire and stared directly at Joseph.

"Will you do it?"

Joseph hesitated.

Tirzah placed a hand on his forearm.

"Do what you have to do, darling. I'll support you."

"Yes, tell Nicodemus I'll do it! By Jerusalem, it is time I stopped skulking about!

"I have a tomb, between Golgotha and the walls, just off the road to Joppa and Emmaus. Tell him to meet me there."

"It will be done, my friends. But we must hurry—there isn't much time to sundown."

"Of course. And Mary?"

"Yes?"

"Thank you."

Mary, called the Magdalene, rushed back to the house where John, Jesus' mother Mary, and Maariah were waiting. A messenger was dispatched to Nicodemus.

"Mary, you and John meet Joseph and his servants at Golgotha," Mary Magdalene said. "I'll go directly to Joseph's tomb. Please forgive me for being so brusque, but we have very little time. Look how long the shadows are."

Mary, the mother of Jesus, her cheeks gaunt and her eyes red from weeping, touched her friend's face.

"Ah, dear, sweet Mary. You are so strong. We will do as you say."

Once at the appointed tomb, Mary waited for long minutes, pacing in worried circles. It was a standard Jewish burial tomb, expertly cut into sheer rock, with a large rolling stone to block the entrance. She anxiously swept the interior several times, trying to burn excess nervous energy.

This is a large, handsome tomb—but hardly the suitable mausoleum for the Son of God! If only there were time, perhaps we could raise the money among Jesus' followers for a bigger, more appropriate tomb! But there's simply no time.

At last, the others arrived. Nicodemus was first, his servants carrying the necessary burial spices, ointments, and fine linen shrouds.

Then came Mary, Joseph, Tirzah, and their servants. They'd loaded the body in a simple wooden cart and brought it with them. Mary, the mother of Jesus, looked dazed.

Mary rushed to her side.

"Is it...bad?"

Mary's eyes slowly focused again and she hugged her friend.

"It is far worse than I imagined," she whispered into Mary's ear. "They...they tortured him, scourged him, beat him horribly, even before they nailed him to that hideous Roman tree."

She broke down again, sobbing uncontrollably.

The friends worked feverishly, bathing Jesus' battered and broken body, cleaning it as best they could. They carefully wrapped him in the beautiful white linen and opened the spices.

But at that moment, bells! Bells from Jerusalem—signalling the beginning of the Sabbath!

Mary pounded her small fist on the unyielding rock.

"No! And we were so close. My Lord, I've failed you again."

Nicodemus gently put his arm around her.

"You've failed no one, my daughter. We'll come back after the Sabbath—at first light—I promise. It is cool in here and I can tell it is well-sealed. It won't make that much difference. Here, come with me."

And with the servants' help, the men struggled to roll the heavy stone, sealing the entrance shut.

Mary stood looking into the darkly shadowed tomb as long as possible.

Good-bye, my Lord. When you found me in Magdala, I was a wealthy woman—but desperately, desperately unhappy. I was inhabited by seven demons, an invalid, bitter, angry, and shrewish.

But somehow, you saw past all of that. And that morning, after teaching all day in the synagogue, you touched me. Healed me. Saved me. Changed me, forever.

Good-bye, my Lord.
Good-bye.

THE GUARDS

To avoid being seen together, the friends broke up and returned to their homes via different routes, at different times.

On Saturday, Simon found himself again outside Pilate's palace, accompanied only by Thomas. Both wore their hoods low over their eyes, obscuring their faces.

"Simon, you idiot! What are we doing here? Someone will see us for sure!"

"Quiet," Simon hissed dangerously, "unless you want to advertise our presence. No one would think to look for us here. Besides, my sources tell me there's about to be another meeting between Pilate and the chief priests. And the priests aren't about to go inside that glorified whorehouse until after the Sabbath."

"So what?" Thomas whispered back. "I don't care if Caesar and Moses are going to meet. It's over! Finished! None of this spy stuff matters anymore. He's dead. Get that through your thick skull, you lame-brained Zealot."

Suddenly, Thomas felt a sharp point, digging into his ribs.

"You'll keep your voice down or I'll silence you myself," Simon said, his voice as cold as steel. "Now listen to me: this thing isn't over—far from it. Jesus raised more than one person from the dead. He kept talking about this 'Sign of Jonah' thing. Think, man! Think about what he said that last night!"

"I think you're grasping at straws—I'm heading out until this thing blows over."

But Simon had already forgotten Thomas. The chief priests and their entourage had arrived. Within moments, Pilate appeared. Only this time, he was genuinely annoyed.

"Now what?!" he thundered at Caiaphas.

Caiaphas knows he's treading on dangerous ground—look how deep he's bowing! Simon thought grimly. *This must be serious for that self-important pig to play the obsequious petitioner.*

"A thousand pardons, oh great governor," Caiaphas said through gritted teeth. "But while this rabble-rouser Jesus of Nazareth was alive, he kept saying, 'I will rise again after three days.' "

"So?"

"So, we're afraid this imposter's disciples will sneak down to the tombs, steal his body away, and tell the fools 'He's risen from the dead!' This second fraud will be worse than the first—and we'll have a full-scale revolt on our hands!"

Pilate cocked an eye at Caiaphas.

"By Zeus, you Jews will be the death of me. You win, priest, but all debts are canceled between us. Take a contingent of guards. Leave a twenty-four-hour watch at the tomb for the next three days. Here, take my centurion Petronius to arrange it."

"Thank you, my lord," Caiaphas said unctuously. "We'll set wax seals about the stone as well."

"Get out of here!"

Simon smiled to himself.

It feeds my soul to see Caiaphas treated like a market beggar. And as for the soldiers, should the king of the universe decide to arise, all the legions of Rome will not keep him in the grave!

Chuckling to himself, Simon headed back toward the safe house.

The safe house, one of several Matthew and Simon had secured in Jerusalem, lay at the end of a dead-end alley, almost in the shadow of the massive, menacing Fortress Antonia. Inside, the surviving disciples milled about aimlessly, hidden behind bolted doors, shivering and shaken. Simon found Peter where he left him, still brooding blackly over his three denials.

Peter glanced listlessly up from staring at his hands.

"Any word?"

"The fools have set a guard about the master's tomb," Simon said jovially.

"What concern is that to us?"

"How can you ask that, Peter?" Simon bounded over to Peter's side. "It means—for the moment anyway—that the stupid priests and Pharisees take the master's return a lot more seriously than you do!"

When Peter didn't answer, Simon grabbed his cloak to leave. "To think he once called you Peter—'The Rock.' "

And then he was gone again.

THE EMPTY TOMB

Sunday morning.
Dawn. Almost.

And in another safe house on the northwest side of Jerusalem, near the three towers, Mary called the Magdalene woke first.

She gently shook those sleeping nearby, Salome, Joanna, and Mary the mother of James.

Salome yawned mightily.

"Oh, Mary—it is still dark. Did you not sleep last night?"

"I slept, but the Sabbath is now past. I want to get to Jesus' tomb as soon as possible and finish the burial preparations."

"Now I know why they call you Mary Magdalene—'magdala' is the Greek form of *mighdol* or watchtower—because you're up and shining while the rest of the world is in the dark!"

Still wiping sleep from their eyes, the four women stumbled down the path to the cemetery, carefully protecting the expensive ointments and oils they carried.

"What shall we do if the Roman guard won't roll the stone back and let us complete our burial preparations?" Joanna asked.

"I...I don't know, I hadn't thought of that," Mary said.

"Oh, don't worry, you'll think of something. You always do."

They rounded the last bend before Joseph's tomb in the pre-dawn mist.

And, suddenly, they stood stock still, stunned, amazed.

The stone was rolled away!

The Roman tent still stood outside the entrance. The Roman guards were still in place, but sleeping soundly, draped over boulders, sprawled like puppets, curled like dogs, in a loose perimeter around the tomb.

Cautiously, all four women entered the expansive tomb.

Mary's heart beat so rapidly and so strongly, she felt it inside her throat and ears.

Inside the tomb, they flinched and cried in fear as one—two men in brilliant white robes sat calmly on a bench where the Master once had lain! Instantly, the four bowed and buried their faces on the ground.

One of the young men spoke, his voice as melodious as a harp. "Do not be afraid. Why do you seek the living among the dead? You seek Jesus of Nazareth, who was crucified. But he is not here. He lives! Come see where he once lay. Now go tell his disciples this: He is going before you to Galilee. You will know the place."

But the four remained on the floor, trembling and shaking with fear.

The angel spoke again, only this time his words were more forceful. "Don't you remember how he told you—even when you were back in Galilee—that the Son of Man must be betrayed into the hands of sinful men and crucified? Don't you remember how many times he told you that he'd rise again? Now go!"

Somehow, Mary found herself outside of the tomb, staggering, blundering her way over the sleeping soldiers. And, followed by the others, she ran at a breakneck pace to the safe home that housed the discouraged, disorganized disciples.

He's gone! He's alive! I think. Maybe they've taken him! But who were those men? Where is he? What's going on? Why is my heart beating so fast? WHAT'S GOING ON?!

At the house, she burst in and found Peter and John already awake. "They have taken the Lord out of the tomb and we do not know where they have laid him!"

John and Peter immediately bolted out the door, leaving the exhausted women gasping for breath. Mary Magdalene looked for a moment at the—mostly—still sleeping disciples, gulped a mouthful of air, then turned to run after them.

John reached the tomb first, still mostly hidden from the first rays of the morning sun. But even from where he stood, he could see the empty burial linen and headpiece, each folded neatly and placed in separate piles.

With Peter's breathless arrival, the two entered the dank tomb.

"They could not have stolen him," John said. "Thieves wouldn't have taken the trouble or the time to fold the burial linen like this. I don't quite understand what this means, but the Master is definitely not here!"

"Let us return, rouse the others, and discuss this," Peter said. "Something is afoot and I'm not sure I understand it."

"And I don't want to be here when these fool soldiers awake—somebody'll blame us for sure!"

They passed Mary on the path.

Mary, panting hard, returned to the empty tomb alone. Suddenly, she heard a clattering of swords and a barrage of Roman curses. She ducked behind a hedge to watch and listen.

Petronius, standing outside his tent, swore at his men and barked orders.

"I'll have you all thrown in the stockade! I'll have you all demoted! I can't believe every man-jack among you fell asleep! Pilate will have my head—but I'll have yours first!" he bawled.

"You three, go and tell Pilate—but for Zeus's sake, wait until he awakens!

"I'll go tell that oily snake Caiaphas myself. You two come with me.

"There's going to be hell to pay here, boys!"

When the soldiers had left, Mary crept out from her hiding place and walked timidly to the tomb. Alone, confused, frightened, she no longer could control her tears. They came in fresh torrents.

Steeling herself, she peered into the tomb one more time.

The same two men, garbed in brilliant, glowing white, were seated on the benches once again.

"Woman, why are you weeping?" one asked. It was a kind, nurturing voice.

Mary replied, "Because they have taken away my Lord, and I do know where they have laid him."

She felt the presence of someone behind her.

A man.

Standing in a shadow, the man asked, "Woman, why are you weeping? Who are you looking for?"

This must be the gardener.

"Sir, if you have carried him away, please tell me where you have laid him, and I will take him away," she replied, her voice beginning to falter.

There is something familiar about this gardener.

The morning sun broke through the olive trees, illuminating the area.

The man smiled and spoke in the voice she'd come to know and love. "Mary."

Merciful Father—it is Jesus!

"Rabboni! Teacher!"

Mary stepped forward to embrace Jesus, but he gently lifted a hand to stop her.

"Do not hold on to me, for I have not yet returned to the Father, Mary. Instead, go and tell my disciples, 'I am returning to my Father and your Father, to my God and your God.' "

Then he disappeared, like the morning mist in the summer sun.

He's alive. He's alive! HE'S ALIVE!

Breathlessly, Mary flew on eagle's wings back to the disciples' safe house a second time. She burst into the little room, only to find the ten still arguing among themselves. They stopped and, of one accord, stared at her.

"I have seen the Lord!

"Didn't you hear me? I HAVE SEEN THE LORD!"

JESUS APPEARS TO THE DISCIPLES

That afternoon, Peter slipped out of the safe house, his mind whirling, spinning with conflicting thoughts. Using Simon's map of back alleys and rooftops, he furtively made his way to check on the house where the women were staying.

On a small rooftop, just a block from the first safe house, Peter was blinded briefly when the sun came out from behind a cloud. When he blinked and opened his eyes, a man was there.

"Excuse me friend, I'm just passing through," Peter said quickly. "I didn't know this was your house, I'll get off imm..."

The man only smiled.

"Jesus? Jesus! JESUS!" Peter shouted.

Jesus waved for Peter to return the way he'd come, then disappeared.

"Master! Don't go! Forgive me. Please..."

He's gone. But he's alive! I must tell the others!

At the other end of the street, a detachment of armored Roman soldiers hastily crawled up a ladder to the rooftops. But when the first one vaulted on to the roof, he saw nothing.

"There's no one here!" he shouted to his commander on the street. "No birds, no washing, and certainly no follower of the Nazarene!"

The commander glared at the merchant standing next to him.

"But I swear I saw the man called Simon Peter on that roof, just seconds ago!" the merchant wailed.

The commander smacked the merchant a resounding blow with his open hand, knocking him off his feet.

"You send us on another wild-goose chase, merchant, and I'll personally throw you in prison!" he thundered.

Late that night, the small band of believers remained paralyzed, locked in a ferocious argument in the safe house.

Simon stood planted in front of the doorway, barring their exit.

"And I'm telling you it is too dangerous for us to leave right now!" he shouted at Peter. "See for yourself. Peek out that window. See that fool with the lantern pretending to sleep? That's one of Caiaphas's men—he's watching this house. For all we know, they may already have Thomas—that's why he hasn't returned."

Peter returned from the window and stood nose to nose with Simon.

"I don't care if there's an army out there. I saw him! Just like I told you! And the angel told Mary to tell us to go to Galilee— and we need to be going! We've already wasted an entire day."

"It's suicide," Simon snarled. "Jesus never taught suicide—unless it was that time he took the three of you atop that mountain."

"Oh, so it's back to that, is it? You've been jealous of me ever since..."

"Oh, would you two knock it off?" Philip groaned. "I can't believe we're arguing over some harebrained report from one hysterical female and Peter's split-second encounter on the roof."

John looked up from his corner. "I saw the empty tomb too, Philip."

"And you believe this business about the angels? You and Peter didn't see any angels."

"I don't know what to believe, Philip."

"Well, I do," Peter roared. "He appeared to me! He indicated that I should return here."

"Then maybe you need to do what the Master says," Simon said quietly.

"No, no—you don't understand! I'm sure he meant that I was to tell the rest of you and that we were to leave for Galilee. Immediately."

A pounding on the barred door caused them all to jump. Simon drew his sword and peered through a slot.

"Yeah?"

"It's me, Cleopas—with Matthias. Let us in—we have wonderful news!"

John looked out the window at the sleeping man.

"It's okay—he's still sleeping—or pretending to be asleep."

"Keep an eye on him while I let these two in."

Cleopas and Matthias tumbled in, their faces flushed, babbling as one.

Peter strode forward.

"One at a time. Cleopas, you first."

"We were walking to Emmaus from Jerusalem," Cleopas gasped. "We were on our way to tell the believers there what had happened—and to warn them that Caiaphas and Annas had ordered a purge."

"Go on, go on!" Peter urged impatiently.

"After a while, a man politely asked if he could joined us, then said, "What are you talking about?"

I said, "Friend, you must be the only visitor to Jerusalem who hasn't heard what's been happening over the past three days."

And he said, "What things?"

"So we told him what had happened to Jesus, and the events of the last few days. We also told him what Mary Magdalene and the other women saw early this morning before we left."

"The man just listened and nodded," Matthias continued, "then he said something peculiar: 'O foolish men, so slow of heart to believe all that the prophets have spoken! Didn't the prophets say that it was necessary that the Christ suffer all of these things before he could enter into glory?'

"Then this stranger did the most amazing thing: he interpreted every Scripture pertaining to the Messiah and attributed it directly to Jesus—including his resurrection!"

John weaved slightly where he stood, as if he might faint. Nathanael alertly brought a chair over to him by the window.

"No, I'm fine, fine," John said. "Cleopas, Matthias, please continue."

"Well, we reached Emmaus, but this man appeared to be going further," Cleopas said. "He was such a charming, learned companion, we begged him to stay with us since the afternoon was growing late. I'd never heard a better teacher.

"We invited him to supper. He took the bread, blessed it, gave it to us, and..."

"...and it was like our eyes were opened!" Matthias interjected excitedly. "It was Jesus! It was Jesus all along!

"HE'S ALIVE, I TELL YOU, ALIVE!"

"Then what, man?" John demanded, now shaking Matthias roughly. "Tell us! Tell us everything!"

"Why, there's not much more to tell. One second he was there, smiling at us, the next he was gone. Vanished.

"I looked at Cleopas and said, 'Man! Didn't our hearts burn within us when he talked to us on the road? Didn't they burn when he opened the Scriptures to us?'"

"We paid our bill and left immediately to return to Jerusalem. We came here as quickly as we could."

"They're telling the truth," Peter said softly. "That's exactly how he appeared to me. It wasn't an illusion, Philip. The same illusion can't happen to three people, miles apart."

"What do you think, Jesus?" Nathanael asked casually.

"Jesus?!"

All quickly spun on their heels, like some fantastic dance troupe. "JESUS!"

And there, standing in the back of the room, beaming at them, stood Jesus of Nazareth, glowing slightly, like coals in a day-old fire.

Some of the disciples fell to the ground. A few stepped back, in fear. "It's a ghost," Thaddaeus whispered.

But Jesus shook his head, and walked forward.

"Why are you troubled, my friends?" he asked gently, soothingly. "Why do you question what you see? See—look at my hands and my feet. You saw what they did to me on that cross. Here, come and touch me. A spirit doesn't have flesh and bones—and wounds like these."

And they crowded around him, touching his wounds, kissing his hands, glorying in the radiance of his light and love.

"There…there are so many questions we have, Lord," Peter stammered. "So much we don't understand. But first, do you have any questions of us?"

"Yes," Jesus said, his familiar smile filling them with warmth. "Do you have anything to eat around here? I haven't eaten in days!"

And after he ate, they reclined around the table and talked long into the night.

And he told them many things, amazing things, of incredible journeys, of impossible sights. He told them of his horrific journey to hell and back, and of the moments in the presence of the Almighty.

"These are the words I spoke to you earlier," he said at last, "that everything written about me in the Law of Moses and the Prophets and the Psalms *must* be fulfilled."

Then he opened their minds to the Scriptures, as he had done with their friends Cleopas and Matthias earlier.

"So it is written," he continued, "that the Christ should suffer and, on the third day, should rise from the dead. In that way, repentance and forgiveness of sins should be preached in my name to *all* nations—beginning from here, tonight. My friends, you witnessed all that I just spoke of. And it will be in Jerusalem that the promise of the Father will come to you, when you will be clothed with power from on high.

"Now, I must go again, for there is much to be done. Leave for Galilee tomorrow, then return shortly to Jerusalem for that hour."

And he was gone.

THE DISCIPLES SURFACE

None of the ten, plus Cleopas and Matthias, could sleep. They spent long hours locked in discussion over what they'd seen and heard. They alternated between praise songs and tears, joyful remembrances, and questions about the wealth of teaching material they'd just heard.

Shortly before dawn, there was another knock at the door. John again peeked out the window. Caiaphas's hapless spy was sprawled out asleep in a most undignified manner. John motioned the "all clear" sign to Simon.

It was Thomas.

"By the Father, where have you been, man?" Simon said. "I've been worried sick!"

"I felt bad about what I said to you at Pilate's palace," Thomas said quickly. "So I decided to do a little sleuthing on my own. And guess what? The tomb is empty!"

"Yes, Thomas, we know. But there's something you should..."

"Wait, there's more!" Thomas said triumphantly. "When the stupid guards met with the priests and elders to tell them that they'd fallen asleep and that Jesus' tomb was empty, they went berserk! I hear, from reliable sources, that the priests ranted and raved and threatened. Then they must have realized—these are Roman soldiers! They can't do a thing to them!"

"Thomas, if you'll just listen..." Simon tried to interrupt.

"Just a minute, just a minute—don't steal my moment in the sun here, you old Zealot! Anyway, the priests finally offered a ton of money to the soldiers and said, 'Tell the people that Jesus' disciples came at night and stole away his body while you were sleeping.' And that's what they've been doing—although it is a stretch to believe that *all* of them were sleeping so soundly that they couldn't have heard that boulder rolled away!

"And you know Petronius—the centurion? He's been sent to Gaul to the front! Wait, there's more..."

"THOMAS, SHUT UP!" Simon roared. "We have seen the Lord! He's been here! He's eaten with us! He's alive!"

Thomas was at first elated, then crestfallen.

"Unless I see the nail marks in his hands and put my fingers where the nails were *and* put my hand in his side, I won't believe it!" he said defiantly. "You're all under some kind of mass hysteria or something."

Peter and John walked up, flanked Thomas, and wrapped their arms around him. "Whatever you say, old friend. Now listen up, there's much to tell you."

When they were through, Thomas sat stone-faced against the back wall.

"You...you all must go on to Galilee without me."

But when they tried to argue, he waved them off.

"It is better this way. I'll watch the safe houses. Then I'll meet you back here in a week."

A few hours later, the remaining ten left for Galilee.

In the days that followed, Jerusalem was aflame with reports of appearances by Jesus—so many that even the remaining disciples couldn't keep up with them. The stories were so pervasive, so wide-ranging, that the Pharisees—temporarily, at least—called off the persecution of Jesus' followers.

Emboldened by the lull, his followers began to surface. At one point, Jesus appeared to a group of nearly five hundred believers. James, Jesus' brother, also reported a personal visitation.

En route to Galilee, the remaining ten spent their days and nights meeting with believers, repeating what Jesus had told them, sending harried messengers with instructions back to Jerusalem.

Word of Jesus' resurrection had spread throughout the land, even to Samaria. Everywhere the ten went, they were welcomed by people hungry for news from Jerusalem.

In Capernaum, they returned to Maariah's house and continued their ministry unhindered by the Pharisees and priests. But Jesus did not appear.

After a few days, Peter told his long-suffering wife, "I suppose I better earn a little money to pay for my keep!" and he left for his fishing boat with the six fishing disciples.

That night's catch was skimpy at best. Exhausted, they returned home.

Early the following morning, they put out once again. While they were still about a hundred yards offshore, a man called out from the beach.

"Ho the boat! Have you caught any fish, my friends?"

"No!" Peter snapped back.

Can't he see our empty nets still draped across the hull?

"Throw your nets off your starboard bow and you will find some," the man shouted.

Impulsively, Peter did just that.

Immediately, the nets filled with fish! The small fishing vessel listed dangerously toward the starboard.

Andrew screamed at Peter, "It's too much! We can't haul the nets back aboard!"

John looked up from his work, peered intently back at the shore, and shouted, "It's the Lord!"

Peter did a double take.

"It is! It is!" he shouted—then jumped in the chilly waters and swam madly toward shore.

The remaining five laboriously turned the fishing boat around and headed toward shore as well, dragging the heavy nets behind them.

On the beach, Jesus had built a roaring fire. Fresh loaves of bread were stacked neatly in nearby baskets.

And when they all had arrived, Jesus said, "Bring some of the fish you have just caught. Then, come—join me for breakfast."

And they did.

When they had finished eating, Jesus leaned forward and said to the still-shivering Peter, "Simon Peter, son of John, do you really love me more than these?"

Peter smiled and said, "Yes, Lord. You know that I love you."

"Good—then feed my lambs."

After a moment, Jesus said again, "Peter, do you truly love me?"

Peter answered, "Yes, Lord, you *know* that I love you."

"Good—then take care of my sheep."

Another awkward pause followed, then Jesus said a third time, "Peter, *do you love me?*"

By now, Peter was hurt and confused and more than a little defensive.

"Yes! Lord—you know all things—you *must* know that I love you!"

Jesus smiled again and sat back. "Then feed my sheep.

"Truly, my friend, when you were young, you dressed your-self and went wherever you wanted to go. But when you get old, you'll have to stretch out your hands and someone else will have to dress you and they will lead you to places you don't want to go."

He's talking about my death—what will happen to me—someday, Peter thought.

Jesus said, "Now, follow me." And he got up and walked down the beach.

As Peter was following, he noticed that John had left the fire as well and was walking at a respectful distance behind them.

"Jesus, what about John? What does the future hold for him?"

"Peter, even if I want him to remain alive until I return—what's that to you? Your job is to follow me."

When they returned from their walk, Jesus summoned all of the disciples in Galilee, told them to make the day's journey to Mt. Tabor—then faded from their view.

When they arrived at the appointed place that afternoon, Jesus was already there! He taught them and prepared them for the heady, dangerous days to come.

They closed in prayer and, when they looked up, he was gone.

JESUS APPEARS TO THOMAS

Emboldened, inspired, and comforted, the disciples returned to Jerusalem.

Then, one week after Jesus' previous appearance in their safe house, the original eleven gathered again in the safe house. As promised, Thomas was there. Simon, cautious as always, locked the door behind them.

The discussion quickly turned to the miracles and appearances of Jesus they'd seen in Galilee.

"Thomas, whether you believe us or not, you should have accompanied us north," Big James said. "That was, more than likely, our last trip together as a group."

"Don't you see—I *want* to believe," Thomas said, his voice on the verge of breaking. "I *want* to have the faith the rest of you have. I *envy* your faith, your confidence. It's just…"

"It's just what, Thomas?" a familiar voice said from the back of the room.

"Jesus! How did you get in here?! I saw Simon lock the door!"

"Oh, Thomas, if the gates of hell couldn't keep me in—do you think a locked door would keep me out?"

Jesus glided over and joined them at the table.

"Peace be with you all," he said.

He stood by Thomas.

"Now, put your finger here—see my hands. Now, reach out your hand and put it in the wound in my side. Are you satisfied, my friend? Now, stop doubting—and believe!"

Thomas groaned and sank to his knees, "Forgive me, my Lord and my God!"

Jesus helped him back to his feet.

"Because you have seen me, you believe. Blessed are those who have not seen and yet believe."

Then, with the first eleven gathered about him, Jesus told them many more incredible things and performed several miraculous signs, strengthening them for the days ahead when he would return to heaven.

After many hours, it was—once again—time for him to leave.

"Peace be with you," he said again. "As the Father has sent me, now I am sending you. Now, do not leave Jerusalem, but wait for the gift my Father promised—which we've talked about in recent days. John baptized you in water, but in a few days, you will be baptized with the Holy Spirit."

In one moment he was there. In the next, he was not.

THE GREAT COMMISSION

Several days later, he appeared to them one last time.

It was now thirty-nine days after his resurrection.

"We shall make one last journey together," Jesus said. "To the Mount of Olives."

As they walked, Simon asked, "Lord, are you now going to restore the kingdom of Israel?"

Nathanael rolled his eyes. "Once a Zealot, always a Zealot."

Jesus just kept walking.

"It is not for you to know the times or dates that the Father has set. But you will receive power when the Holy Spirit comes on you and you all will be my witnesses in Jerusalem, in all Judea and Samaria, and to the ends of the world."

As they began the climb up the Mount of Olives, they passed the Garden of Gethsemane.

Several of the eleven flushed with shame over their cowardly behavior that night, but Jesus never mentioned it.

"At least you got an ear," Simon said glumly to Peter. "I never even got my sword out of my scabbard to defend him!"

"At least you didn't deny him three times that night," Peter answered.

"At least you didn't run all the way to Jerusalem naked!" Nathanael said. "Did you see John Mark that night?"

They laughed, but it was an uneasy, forced laughter.

John whispered back to the three.

"Hey, look at Jesus!"

Walking at the head of their little procession, Jesus seemed to be bathed in an unearthly light.

"It's coming from him," Peter said. "He's glowing."

With each step, Jesus' glow burned brighter. It gradually turned from a warm golden glow to an intense white.

"It's so bright that it should be blinding us, but it's not," John said.

"It's warm—it feels like it is penetrating through me," Thomas said.

"Look!" Nathanael said, laughing. He held his hand up toward Jesus and the light shone through his hand, clearly illuminating all of the bones beneath the skin.

Then they noticed that the sky around them was also turning brighter and whiter. Even the smallest rocks and blades of grass were casting long, sharp black shadows.

"Listen!" Thaddaeus called out. "There's music everywhere."

"It's like thousands of harps and flutes and people singing," Big James said, his eyes wide with wonder.

"Higher, let's go higher!" Little James sang out.

As they neared the gentle summit of the Mount of Olives, the universe around them was gravid with white light and the heavenly sound of voices.

"Simon," Andrew said, "your scars have all healed."

Simon touched his cheek and wept. His tears turned to lovely crystal prisms, casting and reflecting even more of the light.

At the summit, the eleven formed a loose ring around Jesus. One after another, they spread their arms, opened their mouths, closed their eyes—drinking in the liquid light that filled their souls and cleansed their bodies.

And when they opened their eyes, the light shot like a tunnel to heaven.

And they saw the hosts of heaven singing, dancing, flying in ecstatic joy, all welcoming the Son.

In the center of the corridor of light stood Jesus, light pouring out in all directions.

He smiled at each man in turn and said, "My peace be with you always.

"All authority in heaven and on earth has been given to me. Now go, and make disciples of all people, in all nations, baptizing them in the name of the Father, and of the Son, and of the Holy Spirit to come. And teach these new believers everything I've told you and commanded you.

"Then remember this: I will be with you always. Even until the end of the age."

And in that moment, the light grew so dazzling they were forced to close their eyes for a heartbeat.

And when they opened their eyes, a silver cloud surrounded Jesus and carried him to heaven.

Gradually, the light lessened and the music muted. Then it was just the eleven disciples, standing alone atop the windswept mount, still dazed and glowing slightly themselves.

Simon wrenched his eyes from the sky and saw two men in bright white robes standing next to them.

"Who are you?"

The men only smiled and said, "Men of Galilee! Why do you stand looking into the sky? This same Jesus, who has been taken from you into the heaven, will someday return the same way you have seen him leave!"

"Well," said ever-practical Matthew, "I suppose that means it is time for us to leave. There's work to do."

"Tomorrow will be the fortieth day since Jesus rose from the dead," Peter said thoughtfully. "We need to get back to Jerusalem. I have a feeling something wonderful will happen on Pentecost."

And it did.

The Fate of the Twelve

PETER

The fisherman became one of the great missionaries of the new faith, taking the message first among the Jews, then as far as Babylonia to the east and Rome to the west. The first half of the Book of Acts chronicles his evangelistic efforts, and he is credited with writing I and II Peter. Tradition says he was crucified in Rome. But because he felt he was unworthy to be crucified in the same manner as his Lord, he asked that he instead be crucified head downward. His request was granted.

JOHN

John's evangelistic work is said to have centered in Asia Minor, particularly around Ephesus. He stayed with Mary there, the mother of Jesus, until her death—or, as some traditions believe, until her Assumption. His writings include the gospel that bears his name, I, II, and III John, and the Book of Revelation. He was exiled to the Isle of Patmos, was later freed, and died a natural death at an advanced age.

"BIG" JAMES

The brother of John worked mainly in Jerusalem and Judea. He was beheaded by Herod Agrippa about AD 44 (Acts 12:1-2).

ANDREW

Tradition says that Peter's brother, who was originally a disciple of John the Baptist, preached in Scythia, Greece, and Asia Minor. He is said to have been crucified on a St. Andrew's cross.

NATHANAEL

The man who was also called Bartholomew was a missionary to Armenia where tradition says he was flayed to death. Jerome says he wrote a now-lost gospel.

THOMAS

Thomas, also called Didymus, is said to have labored in Parthia, Persia, and India before finally suffering martyrdom near Madras at Mount St. Thomas.

MATTHEW

Also known as Levi, the well-disciplined tax collector is said to have died a martyr in Ethiopia. He is believed to have written the gospel that bears his name.

"LITTLE" JAMES

James may have written the Epistle of James, although many scholars attribute it to James the brother of Jesus. Tradition says that he preached in Palestine and Egypt, where he was crucified.

THADDAEUS

Also known as Jude, he is said to have preached in Assyria and Persia, where he died a martyr. Some traditions claim that he wrote the epistle Jude.

SIMON

Little is known or speculated about the shadowy man known as the Zealot. One tradition says he was crucified, but does not say where.

PHILIP

This quiet native of Bethsaida is rarely mentioned in the biblical narrative and even the post-New Testament legends and traditions are skimpy. There are, however, surviving stories that say Philip preached in Phyrgia and one account claims that he was eventually martyred in Hierapolis.

JUDAS

After betraying Jesus for thirty pieces of silver, Judas hung himself. The priests used the money to buy the land where he died, soon dubbed the Field of Blood.

MATTHIAS

In Acts 1:23-26, Matthias was elected by the apostles to replace Judas, but there is no further mention of him in the Bible. Tradition says he preached and suffered martyrdom in Ethiopia.

SAUL

Later changed his name to Paul and became one of the greatest of all of Jesus' disciples. But that is another story for another time.

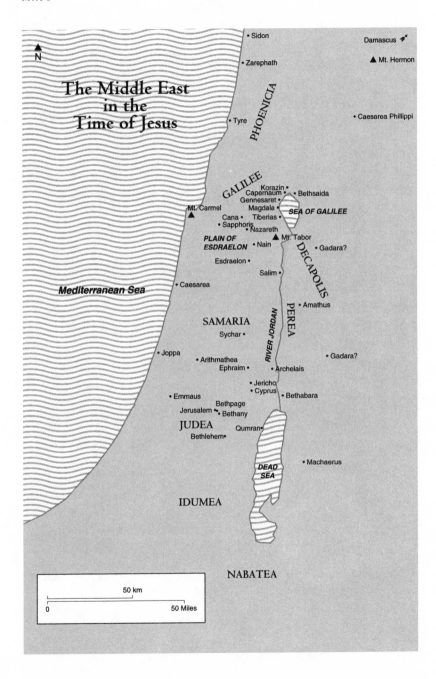

The Middle East in the Time of Jesus

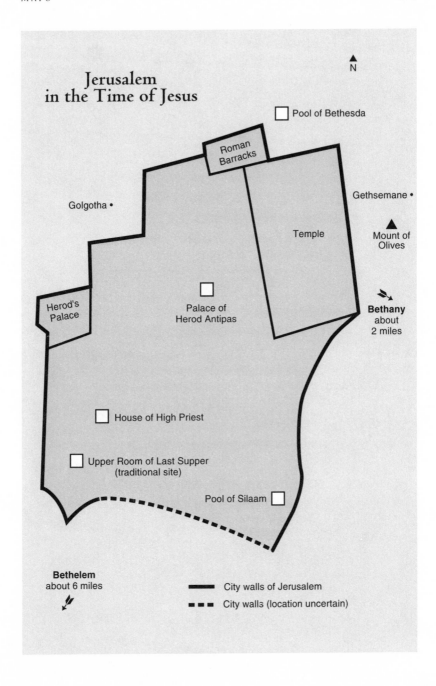

Jerusalem
in the Time of Jesus

N

Pool of Bethesda

Roman
Barracks

Golgotha •

Gethsemane •

Temple

Mount of
Olives

Herod's
Palace

Palace of
Herod Antipas

Bethany
about
2 miles

House of High Priest

Upper Room of Last Supper
(traditional site)

Pool of Silaam

Bethelem
about 6 miles

———— City walls of Jerusalem

▪ ▪ ▪ City walls (location uncertain)